Warrior Prayers

Conversations with God

by
Theda Vaughan

Warrior Prayers

Conversations with God

by

Theda Vaughan

take heart books

Warrior Prayers Conversations with God
Copyright ©2024 *Theda Vaughan*

All rights reserved. No part of this book may be reproduced or used in any manner without written permission from the author, except for the use of quotations in a book review. Send email to theda@warriorprayerbooks.com

ISBN: 978-1-958818-10-7 (paperback)

Published by
Take Heart Books LLC Toledo, OH
Original Cover Art by *Emily Lide*
artwork from Canva

take heart books

Scripture quotations taken from The Holy Bible, New International Version®, NIV® Copyright © 1973, 1978, 1984, 2011 by Biblica, Inc® Used by permission. All rights reserved worldwide.

NIV 1984 The Holy Bible, New International Version. (1984). International Bible Society.

Scripture quotations marked (ESV) are from The ESV® Bible (The Holy Bible, English Standard Version®), © 2001 by Crossway, a publishing ministry of Good News Publishers. Used by permission. All rights reserved.

Scripture quotations marked (NKJV) taken from the New King James Version®. Copyright © 1982 by Thomas Nelson. Used by permission. All rights reserved.

Scripture quotations marked (KJV) from The Authorized (King James) Version. Rights in the Authorized Version in the United Kingdom are vested in the Crown. Reproduced by permission of the Crown's patentee, Cambridge University Press.

Scripture quotations marked (AMPCE) are taken from the Amplified Bible, Copyright © 1954, 1958, 1962, 1964, 1965, 1987 by The Lockman Foundation. Used by permission.

Scripture quotations marked (KJV21) are taken from the 21ST CENTURY KING JAMES VERSION of the Bible. Copyright© 1994 by Deuel Enterprises, Inc. Used by Permission.

Scripture quotations marked (ISV) taken from the Holy Bible: International Standard Version©. Copyright © 1996-2012 by The ISV Foundation. ALL RIGHTS RESERVED INTERNATIONALLY. Used by permission

Scripture quotations marked (MSG) taken from THE MESSAGE. Copyright © 1993, 1994, 1995, 1996, 2000, 2001, 2002. Used by permission of NavPress Publishing Group.

Scripture quotations marked (TPT) are from The Passion Translation®. Copyright © 2017, 2018, 2020 by Passion & Fire Ministries, Inc. Used by permission. All rights reserved. ThePassionTranslation.com

Scripture quotations taken from the (NASB®) New American Standard Bible®, Copyright © 1960, 1971, 1977, 1995, 2020 by The Lockman Foundation. Used by permission. All rights reserved. lockman.org

All Scripture marked with the designation (GW) is taken from GOD'S WORD®. © 1995, 2003, 2013, 2014, 2019, 2020 by God's Word to the Nations Mission Society. Used by permission.

Scripture quotations marked (CSB) are been taken from the Christian Standard Bible®, Copyright © 2017 by Holman Bible Publishers. Used by permission. Christian Standard Bible•, and CSB® are federally registered trademarks of Holman Bible Publishers.

Scripture texts marked (NAB) are taken from the New American Bible, revised edition © 2010, 1991, 1986, 1970 Confraternity of Christian Doctrine, Washington, D.C. and are used by permission of the copyright owner. All Rights Reserved.

Psalm 116:1-2 (TPT)

I am passionately in love with God because he listens to me. He hears my prayers and answers them. As long as I live I'll keep praying to Him, for he stoops down to listen to my heart's cry.

INTRODUCTION

by

Ricky Vaughan

How could I ever be so bold as to come before God and ask him for things or to make requests concerning my life and my family? Is that arrogant? Is it selfish? Is it a "whatever will be, will be" situation or does God want us to be involved in how He works in our lives?

God is waiting and listening for our requests. He wants fellowship and communication with us. In ***Philippians 4:6 (AMP)*** *He says, Do not be anxious or worried about anything, but in everything [every circumstance and situation] by prayer and petition with thanksgiving, continue to make your [specific] requests known to God.*

In every circumstance and situation by prayer and petition with thanksgiving we are to make specific requests known to God! That's very clear! Our Heavenly Father, the God of the universe wants to hear from us…often!

In ***Matthew 7:7-8 (NIV)*** Jesus says –

Ask and it will be given to you; seek and you will find; knock and the door will be opened to you. For everyone who asks receives; the one who seeks finds; and to the one who knocks, the door will be opened.

We are also reminded by Paul in ***Romans 8:32 (NIV)*** that, *He who did not spare his own Son, but gave him up for us all—how will he not also, along with him, graciously give us all things?*

A further point of encouragement in ***Ephesians 3:20 (NIV)*** says, *Now to him who is able to do immeasurably more than all we ask or imagine, according to his power that is at work within us.*

We serve such a big God and a generous God who loves us and wants the best for us! His thoughts are continually on us!

Psalm 139:17 (TPT) *Every single moment you are thinking of me! How precious and wonderful to consider that you cherish me constantly in your every thought!*

This is not just a book about making your requests known to God... But more a book about connecting with God, understanding his will, and praying according to his will. When you pray according to His will, you can't go wrong!

It's a book about agreeing with God. Can you go wrong by agreeing with the Creator of the universe? No! *And this is the confidence that we have toward him, that if we ask anything according to his will, he hears us. And if we know that he hears us in whatever we ask, we know that we have the requests that we have asked of him.* ***1 John 5:14-15 (ESV)***

Why A Warrior Theme?

Why a warrior theme? Why not love and peace and rainbows and flowers? Shouldn't prayer be holy and sweet and reverent? Well…yes. The presence of God is a beautiful and powerful place. A place of refuge and comfort and peace. However, we are also in a war with a real enemy and there is a time to do battle in God's presence with our prayers and intercessions.

There is a thief who has come to steal, kill and destroy in this world. He is going about like a lion testing and prodding to see if he can devour and bring turmoil and destruction into the lives of God's loved ones.

Satan, a finite being, has chosen to go to war with an infinite God. He is small and God is big, so there is no hope for him. He can't attack God, so the best he can do is to attack those God loves. God, in His wisdom has chosen to equip His loved ones with every weapon needed not only to thwart the enemy's advances, but to defeat him every step of the way.

In ***Ephesians 6***, God tells us *to put on the whole armor of God*. **The armor is for warfare.** He instructs us to leave no part of the armor off, to cover every part of ourselves with his protective gear. The whole armor! There is most definitely warfare to be fought in the daily Christian life. The battle has been won! Jesus is victor! But we still must wage war against the enemy. *But in all these things we overwhelmingly conquer through Him who loved us.* ***Romans 8:37 (NASB)***

Your Covenant is Powerful!

It is important to understand that when you made Jesus the Lord of your life, you entered into a covenant with the Eternal God. But what does that mean? *What is a covenant?*

In the ancient middle east, everyone was familiar with covenants. A covenant was a coming together, a commitment or a binding together of two people or groups. If there was a mutual attraction or a mutual need, the two people would choose to enter into an unbreakable agreement. This was a lifelong agreement. It was understood that everything each person had now was available to the other. If you have lack and I have wealth, then neither of us has lack. If you go to war with an enemy, I also go to war with that enemy. That covenant blessing doesn't just reach the two parties, but to all their descendants.

A covenant is a union of joy, not of obligation or dread. We are now joined together. There is no begging. What's mine is yours. If you need strength or weapons to fight your battle, I am there…no questions…I am just there. If you come up short and I have resources, you no longer come up short. From my storehouse comes your supply and blessing. You are now my covenant brother or sister…my life is yours.

A covenant was confirmed over a meal…usually bread and wine. The covenant was also sealed with the shedding of blood, many times a small cut on the hand or wrist and the two parties would bring their hands together, mingling their blood…becoming one flesh. Both members of the covenant would then carry that scar for the rest of their lives. If you met a person and saw that scar, you now know that there is more to this person than meets the eye. Behind him is a covenant partnership…if you deal with him, you also deal with the covenant partner.

So how does all this apply to this book and these prayers? When Jesus shed His blood at the cross and we receive His gift of eternal life, we entered a covenant partnership with Eternal God. We mark, celebrate and remember this covenant with the communion meal.

Now, everything God has is available to us and we must make everything we have, and are, available to God. I know, I know…He got the short end of that deal, but that's what His grace is all about. He takes us and uses us to bring His glory and His kingdom to the earth. And our prayers and decrees help to bring this to pass.

The Real Introduction

In an ideal relationship, every conversation should be an event that brings both individuals closer to each other. Let these prayers be conversations that do just that with you and your Heavenly Father. However, these prayers should also serve to bring God's will in Heaven to your life, your family, your nation and your world. Use these prayers to go deeper into God and His goodness.

CONTENTS

Introduction... viii
Dedication... xv
Page of Honor... xvi

1. *Prayer of Salvation* 1
2. *A Word About Prayer* 3
3. *You Are a Warrior* 5
4. *I Am Your Covenant God* 9
5. *Deepen My Understanding by Spending More Time in Your Presence* 11
6. *God is My Rescuer* 13
   Praise Moment #1 14
7. *God of the Breakthrough!* 15
8. *Whose Report Are You Going to Believe?* 17
9. *Prayer for Forgiveness and Understanding of God's Forgiveness* 19
10. *Don't Let Your Past Define Your Future* 21
11. *Prayer for Healing* 24
12. *Prayer for Children* 27
    Praise Moment #2 29
13. *You Don't Have to be Perfect to be Used by God* 30
14. *Persistent in My Pursuit of God* 32
15. *God is my Problem Solver* 34
16. *Praying and Understanding Your Purpose* 36
17. *Stay Engaged, FIGHT!* 39
18. *Praying Through Anxiety* 41

Warrior Prayers: Conversations with God

Praise Moment #3 . . . . *44*
19. Pray for Peace in the Middle of Grief 45
20. Do Not Doubt My Word 47
21. Desiring the Depths of God 50
22. Pray for the Dreams of Your Heart 52
23. The Extravagance of God 55
24. Show Me That You Are in Details of My Life 57
Praise Moment #4 59
25. Prayer Concerning Weariness 60
26. God is My Victor 64
27. Pray for Understanding that God Pursues You 66
28. Pray for Your Business as a Ministry 68
29. Standing in the Gap 71
30. Prayer for Understanding Faith 74
Praise Moment #5 76
31. Pray for Understanding of How Great God's Love is
   For You and Others 77
32. Prayer Concerning Change 80
33. Prayer to Conquer Fear 82
34. Prayer for Your Spouse 83
35. Dealing With People That Hurt You 85
36. Prayer for Restoration 88
Praise Moment #6 92
37. God is Calling You! 93
38. Prayer for Our Nation 95
39. Praise and Worship 97
40. Engaging Heaven 100
41. Praying for God's Favor 102
Praise Moment #7 . . . . *104*

42. Praying for Israel	105
43. Come Higher	107
44. Accept God's Healing	109
45. God of Miracles	111
Praise Moment #8	*113*
46. Power of Prayer	114
47. How to Pray in the Middle of a Storm	117
48. Help Me, God! I Keep Messing Up.	119
49. Praying to Overcome Loneliness	122
50. Overcoming Obstacles	125
51. Hearing God's Voice	127
52. Confidence in Victory	129

About Theda... cxxxi

DEDICATION

To my husband who always encourages me to listen to heaven...
Who always cheers me on and who is the rock of our family...
We are truly blessed with your wisdom, your guidance and your love. I am so thankful God put us together.
Together we shall accomplish great things for the Kingdom of God!

PAGE OF HONOR

Ricky and I want to deeply thank our pastors, ***Thomas and Edna Jones***, of Solid Ground Ministries. They have been our pastors and friends for decades. They have exemplified what it means to love and to never compromise the Word of God. Daily they have instilled in those around them a compassion to help, love and minister to others. Their heart for the salvation of the lost is unparalleled. Their passion for Praise and Worship is like none we've ever seen. They have a deep desire for all to experience the depths of the Lord.

Thomas and Edna, we thank you for your encouragement over the years, we thank you for your consistency in reminding us that "Failure is not an option." Thank you for demonstrating a *never give up* attitude. Without that, this book might have never been published. You are true Warriors for the Kingdom and we are proud to call you friends and pastors.

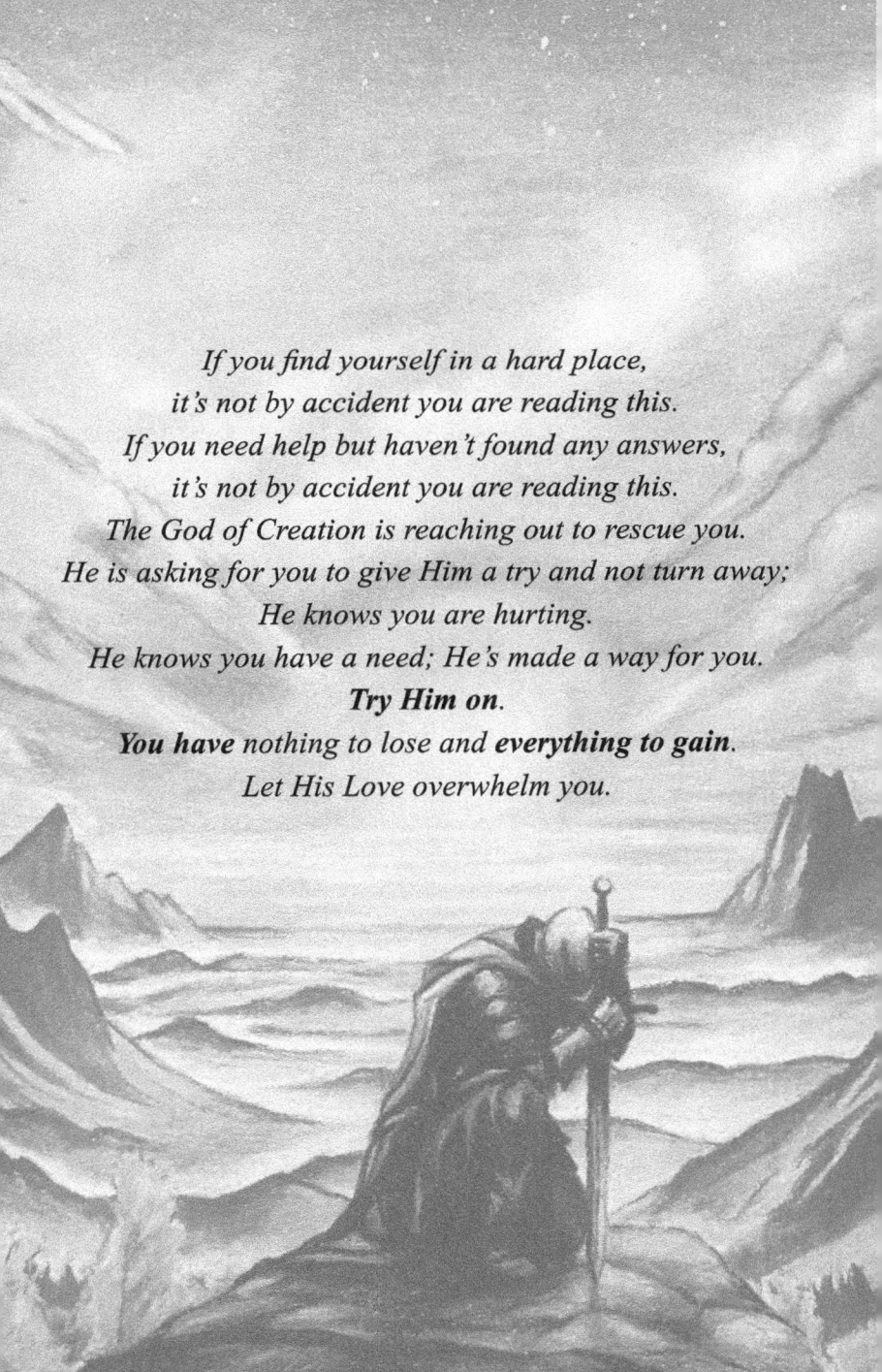

*If you find yourself in a hard place,
it's not by accident you are reading this.
If you need help but haven't found any answers,
it's not by accident you are reading this.
The God of Creation is reaching out to rescue you.
He is asking for you to give Him a try and not turn away;
He knows you are hurting.
He knows you have a need; He's made a way for you.*
Try Him on.
You have *nothing to lose and* **everything to gain**.
Let His Love overwhelm you.

1

PRAYER OF SALVATION

For God so loved the world that...

Before you begin to read and speak these warrior prayers, you must make sure you are indeed part of God's family. *You are not reading this book by accident.* It is a divine appointment for you to meet your Creator God. If you have never asked Jesus to be the Lord of your life and come live in your heart, then God wants you to know, that He loves you so much, he let his only son, Jesus, suffer and die on the cross for you and your sins. Then he went into the pit of hell and defeated Satan and his cohorts, making a way for you to go to heaven and live in a perfect eternity with Him. *Jesus laid down His life for you.* He endured great suffering for you. He made a way for you to walk in victory in your day-to-day life because he knows the challenges you face. He made a way for you to be healed, he made a way for you to be rescued from where you are right now, no matter what you have done or are doing, in your life. His love is so great that it conquered everything just for you. There is nothing you have done that is too big or so bad that he cannot forgive. He stands here, right now, with open arms stretched out to you, asking you to receive him. It's very simple. So please, if you have not asked Jesus into your heart and asked him to be the Lord of your life, do so now, by saying these words out loud:

Father God, I know I have done many things that are wrong and that I am a sinner, and I ask for Your forgiveness. I believe Your son died for me on the cross and rose from the dead. I choose to turn away from my sins and ask Jesus to come into my heart and life.

Jesus, I want to trust and follow You as my Lord and Savior. I want to be all you created me to be.

Thank you, Jesus, for coming into my heart. 𝔄men.

John 3:16 (NIV) For God so loved the world that he gave his one and only Son, that whoever believes in him shall not perish but have eternal life.

2

A WORD FROM THE LORD ABOUT PRAYER

Let my Love pull you into prayer...

*My Child, I am your only hope, not your last resort!
Prayer should be a vital and intricate part of your life.
It is your lifeline. Without prayer you cannot connect to
me. Without prayer you are choosing to live a substandard life. Without prayer you have no power over the
enemy.*

*It is critical that you have communication with me daily. Life's issues are far too great for you to go it alone. I
did not create you to go it alone. I created you to commune with Us (Father, Son and Holy Spirit). The enemy
throws arrows and darts at you everyday to defeat you
and keep you from moving forward. The enemy does
not want you to spend time in prayer, but...*

Prayer cuts through the noise and allows you to hear.
*When you pray you can hear my heartbeat. When you
pray you can hear my desires for you. You can hear the
plans that I have for you, your family, your business or
job. The noise of life is very loud. Prayer cuts through
the noise and allows you to hear me. I am the one with
all your answers, I am the one that gives direction and
guidance. I am the one who knows your beginning from
your end. Why would you choose not to pray? It is a
foolish thing to not pray. The lost and doers of evil do
not pray. Why would you be like them?*

*Connecting with me gives definition to your life that
you wouldn't have any other way. You get direction,*

guidance and revelation. You get comfort and peace when you connect with me. Prayer is not something that should be casual. It should not be something you do when you get a minute. Communication with me should be intentional and purposeful, full of expectation that you have connected with heaven, you have connected to your creator, you have connected with your Savior. Why would you just do that because you get a minute?
Let my love pull you into prayer. If you haven't been spending time with me, don't condemn yourself, but draw unto me. My love is pulling you into my presence. Don't ignore it. Embrace it. I have so much for you to know and understand. I have so many blessings to pour out, but if you're not connected, you will miss my blessings. You cannot find out who I am at my depths without prayer. You must dive deep. The abundance of life is in the deep, the understanding of my extreme love and compassion is in the deep. Your protection is in the deep. Follow me into the depths. Says your Lord!

Father, teach me to pray. Draw me close to you. Let prayer be *my go-to* in every situation and not my last resort. As I enter into your presence, as I pray these prayers, let me hear your voice, let me feel your love for me and understand your love and compassion for others.

In Jesus' name. 𝔄𝔪𝔢𝔫.

3
YOU ARE A WARRIOR
Take the helmet of salvation, and the sword of the spirit...

It is clear, if you are in God's kingdom, YOU ARE A WARRIOR. God is specific in telling us that we have an adversary. Even though we have an adversary, God has equipped us to overcome that adversary. (*Your enemy, the devil, prowls around like a roaring lion looking for someone to devour.*) He has also enabled us able to avoid his tactics and strategies. God gave us His armor. If we aren't warriors in God's kingdom, why would we need armor? We wouldn't.

While we never want to give Satan and his minions credit for anything, God is clear that we wrestle not with flesh and blood (people), but with principalities. *Eph. 6:12 (NIV) For our struggle is not against flesh and blood, but against the rulers, against the authorities, against the powers of this dark world and against the spiritual forces of evil in the heavenly realms. 1 Peter 5:8 (NIV) Be alert and of sober mind. Your enemy the devil prowls around like a roaring lion looking for someone to devour.* Many Christians don't think about the spirit realm and the battle that is constantly occurring. We are to engage with heaven in prayers, praise, worship and wielding our sword. This is how you fight your battle and help others fight theirs. Put on your armor, pray and wield your sword. (THE WORD)

Many Christians also think that whatever happens is God's will. **Stop and really think about that**. Is it God's will for child trafficking to take place, for murder and rapes to take place? NO! Do not confuse the actions of the enemy with God's will. Without going into an in-depth teaching on this subject, just know that in the beginning, Satan deceived Eve into eating the fruit and Adam willfully ate of the fruit that God said not to eat of. When that happened, Adam gave the authority of the earth that God had given him (Adam), over to Satan; over to darkness. But God made a way for us to defeat evil and return our authority to us through Jesus. Praise God, through Jesus we have the victory.

However, we must act. This book is a tool for you to engage with heaven, using your authority to defeat darkness in your life, in your family's life and even in your nation.

Eph. 6:10-18 (AMP) In conclusion, be strong in the Lord [draw your strength from Him and be empowered through your union with Him] and in the power of His [boundless] might. Put on the full armor of God [for His precepts are like the splendid armor of a heavily-armed soldier], so that you may be able to [successfully] stand up against all the schemes and the strategies and the deceits of the devil.

For our struggle is not against flesh and blood [contending only with physical opponents], but against the rulers, against the powers, against the world forces of this [present] darkness, against the spiritual forces of wickedness in the heavenly (supernatural) places.

Therefore, put on the complete armor of God, so that you will be able to [successfully] resist and stand your ground in the evil day [of danger], and having done everything [that the crisis demands], to stand firm [in your place, fully prepared, immovable, victorious].

So stand firm and hold your ground, HAVING [a]TIGHTENED THE WIDE BAND OF TRUTH (personal integrity, moral courage) AROUND YOUR WAIST and HAVING PUT ON THE BREASTPLATE OF RIGHTEOUSNESS (an upright heart), and having [b]strapped on YOUR FEET THE GOSPEL OF PEACE IN PREPARATION [to face the enemy with firm-footed stability and the readiness produced by the good news]. Above all, lift up the [protective] [c]shield of faith with which you can extinguish all the flaming arrows of the evil one.

And take THE HELMET OF SALVATION, and the sword of the Spirit, which is the Word of God. With all prayer and petition pray [with specific requests] at all times [on every occasion and in every season] in the Spirit, and with this in view, stay alert with all perseverance and petition [interceding in prayer] for all [d]God's people.

This is spiritual armor, not natural armor. When we wield our sword against our enemy it is not a blade of steel and iron, but a blade that is sharper than any natural two-edged sword. **IT IS THE WORD OF GOD!**

While there are several pieces of your Armor, this book focuses on your Sword. (The Word of God.) Your sword is your offensive, *and defensive*, weapon. It is always better to be in an offensive posture than to be in a defensive posture. Your sword, the Word of God, can be used in time of trouble and can be used against the enemy with success. It must be used **daily** to keep the enemy away before he is successful at disrupting things in your life and the lives of others.

This is why the prayers you are about to read and **SPEAK OUT LOUD** are deemed Warrior Prayers! When Satan tempted Jesus in the wilderness, **JESUS SPOKE "IT IS WRITTEN"** this is Jesus wielding the Sword of the Spirit. This is our EXAMPLE.

We are in the army of God; we have our defensive and offensive weapons, and we are not to let them sit idle. We are to be fully adorned with His Armor. We are to continually wield the Sword of the Spirit. **Being in the army of God is not passive. It is active.** The kingdom of darkness would love to win over the Kingdom of Light. The enemy can only win if we are passive and refuse to engage in the battle over darkness.

Be a Warrior, be active, knowing that the Lord God Almighty will lead you successfully to victory!

4

I AM YOUR COVENANT GOD

The Lord your God is God; he is the faithful...

Deut. 7:9 (NIV) Know therefore that the Lord your God is God; he is the faithful God, keeping his covenant of love to a thousand generations of those who love him and keep his commandments.

Hebrews 13:20-21 (NIV) Now may the God of peace, who through the blood of the eternal covenant brought back from the dead our Lord Jesus, that great Shepherd of the sheep, ²¹equip you with everything good for doing his will, and may he work in us what is pleasing to him, through Jesus Christ, to whom be glory for ever and ever. Amen.

A Word from the Lord to You

My Child, I AM your Living God. I AM your Covenant God. I am the God of Great Expectations. One of my greatest desires is for you to truly understand the covenant relationship that I have for you, ushering in the manifestation of the great expectations I have for you. The power of my love, solidified by my covenant, is extreme power; it is extreme blessing; it is extreme wisdom, knowledge and understanding. Everything you do is wrapped up in my extreme covenant. But you do not understand. I need you to understand. I need you to search deep within yourself and deep within my Word for the understanding of what my covenant actually means and does for you. Because with that knowledge, your life will flow much differently than it currently does. If your life is great now, it can be even greater. If you are struggling through life, understanding the meaning of our covenant together will get you through to the other side. If you are drowning with the issues of life, it is your life preserver. You are sealed by an unbreakable Blood Covenant. Being in covenant with Me means, all that I am is yours and all that you are is mine. It means, your weaknesses and short comings become mine and my strength and weapons are yours. There is an exchange of identity, you are now in Me and I am now in you. Just as I did for Abraham and Sarah; when I made covenant with them, My identity changed to the God of Abraham and the God of Sarah., and that's when I changed their names and identity to represent Me by changing their names from Abram and Sarai to Abraham and Sarah because I breathed my covenant breathe into them. Even your heirs and descendants are included in this covenant. I need you to grasp hold that all of Me, the Great I AM, is in you. My power, My peace, My healing, My Love, My victories, My wisdom. The list is infinite because I am infinite. With this understanding you will realize that I am the God who has great expectations for you. As you pray these prayers always remember that you are activating your covenant rights. My covenant cannot be broken. Keeping your covenant connection in the forefront of your daily life will be life changing. Let this thought be branded into your mind; I AM THE GOD OF _____ (put your name here).

Expect great things, for I am Great, says your Covenant God!

5

DEEPEN MY UNDERSTANDING BY SPENDING MORE TIME IN
YOUR PRESENCE

For the Lord gives wisdom...

Father, I come before you today asking that as I go deeper in you, You become more alive within me. Your Word says in *Matt. 16:19 (NIV), "I will give you the keys of the kingdom of heaven; whatever you bind on earth will be bound in heaven, and whatever you loose on earth will be loosed in heaven."*

Therefore, I bind distractions from keeping me from spending time with you. I am determined to not let anything—work, family, friends or any activity—come before my time with you. I desperately seek wisdom, knowledge, understanding and discernment so that I might live a life that is pleasing to you and helpful to those around me. Constantly remind me that my actions, or lack of actions, can stop or stifle my forward progress or even cause me to go backwards. I acknowledge that my family, friends, coworkers, employees, etc., can be impacted positively or negatively based on how strong my relationship is with you. Your Word says, in *Prov. 3:5-6 (NIV) Trust in the LORD with all your heart and lean not on your own understanding; in all your ways submit to him, and he will make your paths straight.*

So, Lord, I choose to submit to you and not lean to my understanding, but to lean to Yours. Father, help me to be the person you created me to be. Fulfilling the hope and future you have for me. *Jeremiah 29:11 (NIV) "For I know the plans I have for you," declares the L*ORD*, "plans to prosper you and not to harm you, plans to give you hope and a future."*

Father, I refuse to leave anything on the table. I will not compromise; I will not give in; I will not get distracted; I will not give up; I will not be swayed by whatever life throws at me to stop seeking you with all my heart. I know wisdom and knowledge come from You. *Proverbs 2:6 (NIV) For the L*ORD *gives wisdom; from his mouth comes knowledge and understanding.*

I know that I desire your voice to be the loudest voice I hear. I desire Holy Spirit to be active in every detail of my life, whether personally and/or professionally. I will walk the path you created for me in its perfectness, because I choose to keep my eyes upon you.

I am not going to let the enemy steal my time with You. *John 10:10 (NIV) The thief comes only to steal and kill and destroy; I have come that they may have life and have it to the full.*

The enemy is a thief. He will not steal from me. He will not steal my time, he will not steal Your best for me and my family. He will not steal anything from me.

I am determined to seek you every day, LORD.

Every day I will hear Your voice.

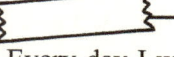

Every day I will obey your voice and every day I choose YOU first.

6
GOD IS MY RESCUER

He reached down from on high and took hold of me...

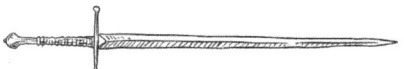

Father, your Word shows that you are my Rescuer, that the greatest rescue you performed was at the cross. You rescued me from death, hell and the grave. *Psalm 18:16-29* shows how You rescued me from my strong enemy. You rescue me from those who hate me. You rescue me from those who are too strong for me. When I am weak and in distress you rescue me.

Father, help me to recognize you as my Rescuer. That no matter what I face I can depend on you to be there for me. I can depend on the guidance of Holy Spirit to lead and direct me. I can depend on your Word to also direct me. Show me in your Word the answer to whatever issue I face. If my body needs rescuing, I will decree healing scriptures over my body. If I need peace, I will decree peace scriptures over my life. If I need resources such as finances, people, or anything to do with providing a need, I will decree what your Word says about it. I agree with your Word.

Father, because you are your Word, I will saturate myself in your Word knowing that you are my Rescuer and that with you, all things are possible.

In Jesus' name. 𝔄𝔪𝔢𝔫.

PRAISE MOMENT #1

Father, I want to stop and just give you thanks.
I don't want to ask you for anything.
I just want to enter your presence with thanksgiving.
I want to thank you for your promise to never leave me nor forsake me.
I want to thank you for coming to give me life, and give it more abundantly.
I want to thank you that I can come and abide in you. Thank you that you are my Refuge and my Rock in whom I trust.
Thank you that you are with me, therefore, who can be against me.
Thank you that every good and perfect gift comes from above.
Thank you for your wonderous works.

Psalm 28:7 (ESV) The Lord is my strength and my shield; in him my heart trusts, and I am helped; my heart exults, and with my song I give thanks to him.

Isaiah 12:4 (ESV) Give thanks to the Lord, call upon his name, make known his deeds among the peoples, proclaim that his name is exalted.

7
GOD OF THE BREAKTHROUGH!

The Lord will fight for you: you only need to be still...

Thank you, Father, that you are the God of the breakthrough! Thank you that no matter how tough things get, I can be of good cheer because I know you are the God of the Breakthrough. You have given me everything I need to break through whatever comes against me or my family.

Lord, one of your names is Jehovah Perazim, *The God of the Breakthrough*. You gave us your different names throughout the Word to show us your many different traits. What a powerful promise. You are the **God of the Breakthrough.**

Today, Lord, I have several things where I need to experience a breakthrough:

1. I have been praying for a long while for _____ _____.
2. Today, I come to you asking for things to change, for there to be movement in _____.
3. Today, I choose to praise You throughout the day that you are Jehovah Perazim.
4. Give me knowledge to understand what part I need to play to move to breakthrough in my life.

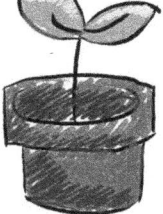

Father, in *Exodus 14:14 (NIV)* your word says, *The Lord will fight for you: you only need to be still.*

You were telling the Israelites that their breakthrough was coming. Their Victory was at hand. Lord, you had let the Israelites see your powerful hand many, many times as they were being delivered from the hands of the Egyptians. You were telling them to be still and let you fight for them.

Father, help me to have the confidence to let you fight for me. When I've done all I can do, then I will stand because you are the Lord my God, and You are with me. *Ephesians 6:13-14 (NIV)* declares, *Therefore put on the full armor of God, so that when the day of evil comes, you may be able to stand your ground, and after you have done everything, to stand. Stand firm then, with the belt of truth buckled around your waist, with the breastplate of righteousness in place.*

8

WHOSE REPORT ARE YOU GOING TO BELIEVE?

And the peace of God which surpasses all understanding...

𝔉ather, many times when I come before you it's hard to truly understand what I am going through. Sometimes I face things that seem insurmountable. I am experiencing one of those times now. I received a bad report, Lord, and as I search your Word for answers, I notice that Your Word asks me a question in Isaiah 53:1. It asks, Whose report am I going to believe? In Isaiah, when that question was asked to your people, you had just given them prophecies of restoration and redemption. Prophecies of blessings and victories even though they had been going through captivity and destruction.

Please help me to remember that throughout Your Word you have made promise after promise concerning all the issues I face. Your Word says that I can have victory, that I can have understanding. Your Word says in *Luke 1:37 (KJV), For with God nothing shall be impossible.*

So whose report am I going to believe?

Whose report are you going to believe?

I will believe Your report, Lord.

Today, I choose to the **think, say and believe** like You do. When the doctor says I am sick, I will give your report that says **BY THE STRIPES OF JESUS I AM HEALED.** *Isaiah 53:5 (NKJV) But He was wounded for our transgressions, He was bruised for our iniquities; The chastisement for our peace was upon Him, And by His stripes, we are healed.*

When there is chaos all around me and my mind is in turmoil, I will believe your report that says You are the God that gives me peace that passes all understanding. *Philippians 4:7 (ESV) And the peace of God, which surpasses all understanding, will guard your hearts and your minds in Christ Jesus.*

No matter what the report is, LORD, whether it is a loss, lack, sickness, anxiety or fear, your Word is true and I choose to believe your promise in *Psalm 34:19 (NKJV) Many are the afflictions of the righteous, but the LORD delivers us out of them all.*

I pray for deliverance today, LORD, in accordance with your Word.

Thank you for the victory!

By the Stripes of Jesus I am Healed!

9
PRAYER FOR FORGIVENESS AND UNDERSTANDING OF GOD'S FORGIVENESS

There is now no condemnation for those who are...

1 John 1:9 (NIV) If we confess our sins, he is faithful and just and will forgive us our sins and purify us from all unrighteousness.

Col. 3:13 (NIV) Bear with each other and forgive one another if any of you has a grievance against someone. Forgive as the Lord forgave you.

Eph. 1:7 (NIV) In him we have redemption through his blood, the forgiveness of sins, in accordance with the riches of God's grace.

Romans 4:7-8 (NIV) Blessed are those whose transgressions are forgiven, whose sins are covered. Blessed is the one whose sin the Lord will never count against them.

A Word from the Lord to You

Forgiveness is My heartbeat. Without forgiveness we could not have a relationship. My heart's desire is to have a relationship with you, an intimate relationship with you and sin separates us from that. When you asked me to be the Lord of your life, I immediately took your sins away. That is why you felt such a weight lift off you on that glorious day that you received Me. Now, as you walk through this life as my child, you have an internal compass that points to right and wrong so that you do not fall into your old ways. 2 Cor. 5:17 Therefore, if anyone is in Christ, he is a new creation; old things have passed away; behold, all things have become new. Holy Spirit leads you toward righteousness when you are about to sin or go against my Word. Holy Spirit prompts you to stay away from things that could be dangerous for you or your family. The enemy tries to tell you all the things you have done wrong or could have done better. That is his way. He goes about like a roaring lion seeking whom he MAY devour. One of his tricks is to bring on condemnation. But I say to you in Romans 8:1 Therefore, there is now no condemnation for those who are in Christ Jesus. If you have sinned, my child, bring that sin before me and ask for forgiveness, then turn away from that sin. Do not go back to your old ways. Please understand, it is my greatest joy when my children turn to me for help, whether you are asking for forgiveness or something else, I want to help you, I want to deliver you, I want to forgive you and set you on the right path. Do not run from me, but run toward me. Your answer is in Me. You cannot do anything so big that I cannot forgive. You've never done anything that has surprised me and you never will. Remember the example of David. I told him he was a man after my own heart! David was a murderer. Yahweh Hessed is one of my many names, this name means God of Forgiveness. You cannot separate me from who I am. I am the God who Forgives. Do come boldly to me today and confess your sin and turn away from that sin. Then let us walk hand in hand together to Victory.

Father, thank you for your Word to me. Thank you, you are full of compassion and mercy. Thank you that your forgiveness restores and renews me and allows me to move forward. Father, I choose this day to stop and turn away from the things I am doing that are not pleasing to you. I ask you to forgive me and help me to walk upright, doing the things I know that are right. Lead and guide me to become more like you every day.

In Jesus' name. Amen.

10

DON'T LET YOUR PAST DEFINE YOUR FUTURE

For I know the plans I have for you....

Hebrews 8:12 (ESV) For I will be merciful toward their iniquities, and I will remember their sins no more.

Romans 8:1 (ESV) There is now no condemnation for those who are in Christ Jesus.

Joshua 1:9 (NKJV) Be strong and of good courage; do not be afraid, nor be dismayed, for the Lord your God is with you wherever you go.

A Word from the Lord to You

My child, listen intently to me today! You are still living in the failures of your past. You rehearse them every day. You are allowing your past to pull you down like quicksand. Your thoughts are smothering you, almost paralyzing you from moving forward. I need you to stop! You asked Me to forgive you and I have. Now, it's time for you to forgive yourself. It's time for you to move forward. It's time to let me pull you out of the quicksand that is trying to destroy you. Stop living in your past and choose to live in your future. This will be your pivot point to Victory. One of the enemy's most powerful tools is attacking your mind. He is great at heaping condemnation on you, suggesting that what you have failed at in the past will keep continuing forward into your future. IT

WILL NOT! But you must trust Me. You must replace the enemy's thoughts and your thoughts of failure, with My thoughts. My thoughts are only good toward you. Doesn't my Word say that you can do all things through Christ who strengthens you? It does not say that you failed once so of course you will fail again. NO, NO, NO. You need to have the mindset that failure is not an option, because you serve the risen King. You serve the Great I Am and you have the Creator of the universe residing on the inside of you, guiding you in all your ways, if you will take heed and listen. You can learn from failure, of course, but learning from failure and falling into condemnation because of failure are vastly different. My Word says there is NOW no condemnation to those who are in Christ Jesus. Now is NOW. I need you to walk in the Now. Believing you will get through this because of my power working in you. My Power! The same power that raised people from the dead, opened blind eyes, healed multitudes of people. That is the power that you have inside of you. Now pull out your Sword (My Word) and demand that the enemy leave your mind. Tell him he will be unsuccessful at condemning you. Remind the enemy who and whose you are. He hates that!!! Remember failure is not the end of your story. I have great things in store for you! Decree what My Word says over yourself!

Psalm 37:23-24 (NLT) You, Lord, direct my steps for I am godly. You delight in every detail of my life. Though I stumble, I will never fall, for you Lord hold me by the hand.

2 Cor. 4:8-9 (NLT) When I am pressed on every side by troubles, I will not be crushed. When I am perplexed, I will not be driven to despair. I am hunted down, but never abandoned by you God. I might get knocked down, but will not be destroyed.

Prov. 24:16 (NIV) For though the righteous fall seven times, they rise again, but the wicked stumble when calamity strikes.

Romans 8:28 (NIV) And I know that in all things God works for the good of those who love him, who have been called according to his purpose.

Micah 7:8 (NIV) Do not gloat over me, my enemy! Though I have fallen, I will rise! Though I sit in darkness, the Lord will be my light.

Phil. 4:13 (NIV) I can do all this through Him who gives me strength.

Isaiah 41:10 (NLT) I will not be afraid, for You are with me. I will not be discouraged, for you are My God. You will strengthen me and help me. You will hold me up with your victorious right hand.

Jeremiah 29:11 (NLT) "For I know the plans I have for you," says the Lord. "They are plans for good and not for disaster, to give you a future and a hope."

Thank you, Lord, for your Word.

I choose to keep your Word at the forefront of my mind.

If I hear my old thoughts creeping in, I will cast them down because, You, God, the Great I AM, live boldly in me.

In Jesus' name. 𝔄𝔪𝔢𝔫.

11
PRAYER FOR HEALING

Wherefore take unto you the whole armour of God...

1 Peter 2:24 (KJV) Who his own self bare our sins in his own body on the tree, that we, being dead to sins, should live unto righteousness: by whose stripes ye were healed.

James 5:14-15 (NIV) Is anyone among you sick? Let them call the elders of the church to pray over them and anoint them with oil in the name of the Lord. And the prayer offered in faith will make the sick person well; the Lord will raise them up. If they have sinned, they will be forgiven.

Psalm 103:2-3 (NIV) Praise the Lord, my soul, and forget not all his benefits— who forgives all your sins and heals all your diseases.

Matthew 10:1 (NIV) Jesus called his twelve disciples to him and gave them authority to drive out impure spirits and to heal every disease and sickness.

Matthew 16:19 (MSG) "And that's not all. You will have complete and free access to God's kingdom, keys to open any and every door: no more barriers between heaven and earth, earth and heaven. A yes on earth is yes in heaven. A no on earth is no in heaven."

Matthew 16:19 (NKJV) And I will give you the keys of the kingdom of heaven, and whatever you bind on earth will be bound in heaven, and whatever you loose on earth will be loosed in heaven.

Mark 11:23 (NKJV) For assuredly, I say to you, whoever says to this mountain, 'Be removed and be cast into the sea,' and does not doubt in his heart, but believes that those things he says will be done, he will have whatever he says.

Father, in the name of Jesus, I come before you today speaking and believing your Word, that by the stripes of Jesus I am healed. Speaking that the enemy has no power over my body. You have given me authority to overcome the enemy who has come to steal, kill and destroy. Today I use the authority you gave me to bind the enemy off of my body. Satan and his cohorts will be unsuccessful at keeping me ill. I speak the Word that says the enemy is defeated by the blood of the Lamb and word of my testimony. My testimony is: **BY THE STRIPES OF JESUS I AM HEALED**. My testimony is that no weapon formed against me shall prosper; my testimony is that nothing is impossible with God. Your Word says plainly that whatever I bind on earth is bound in heaven and that whatever I loose on earth is loosed in heaven. Therefore I bind Satan and all his demons, all the powers and rulers of the darkness and spiritual wickedness in high places, off of my body and I loose all of heaven to come to my defense to assure my healing.

Father, the Word is full of scriptures that promise healing. Jesus, you used the Word against the enemy while he was tempting you. You were the Word speaking the Word, and as a child of yours, I am joint heirs with Jesus, so I speak your word boldly with great expectation that I am healed. I choose to speak the healing scriptures found in your Word over me again and again for as long as it takes.

Now I stand with the knowledge that Greater are You that is in me than he that is in the world and by the stripes of Jesus I am healed. In Jesus' Mighty Name. 𝔄men.

Eph. 6:13 (KJV) Wherefore take unto you the whole armour of God, that ye may be able to withstand in the evil day, and having done all, to stand.

Make sure you are speaking the Word while you stand!

12

PRAYER FOR YOUR CHILDREN

Children are a gift from the LORD...

𝔉ather, in the name of Jesus, I lift up my children to you this day and as always I ask for protection over their lives. Your Word says that you give your angels charge over us.

Psalm 91:11-12 (NKJV) For He shall give His angels charge over you, To keep you in all your ways. In their hands they shall bear you up, Lest you dash your foot against a stone.

Psalm 127:3 (NLT) says, *Children are a gift from the LORD.* Therefore Lord, they are so precious to you, I ask they be steered to walk in success and to desire to serve you with their whole hearts. I ask they be not swayed by the trappings of the world, but that you become *and stay* their compass. I cover them with the blood of the Lamb which has destroyed the enemy, and we are victorious over the enemy because of that blood and the word of our testimony. My testimony today is that by the stripes of Jesus my children are healed. My testimony today is that no weapon formed against them will prosper. My testimony today is that every demonic strategy be thwarted from their lives. I pray that you keep evil doers out of their lives and that you will send godly people with only good intentions into their lives. I pray they will be givers and not takers, that they will follow the leading of the Holy Spirit daily and the voice of a stranger they will not listen to. I pray that your voice will be the loudest voice they hear as they make life decisions, whether those decisions are about school, friendships, spouses, job opportunities or where they will worship. Teach them compassion and kindness for all people. Let them learn their life lessons with you as their foundation. In all their actions and deeds, let them know that the one and only true Living God is for them and never against them.

In Jesus' name, I pray. Amen.

PRAISE MOMENT #2

Thank you, Father, that I can enter into your throne room.
I can experience your glory, knowing how much you love me.
Thank you for Jesus, for my salvation.
Thank you, Holy Spirit, that you are my compass.
Thank you, Father, for your plan of redemption made from the foundations of the earth.
What a love story!
You allowed your only Son to be crucified so that I might have eternal life with you.
I thank you deep within my soul that you made a way.
You are truly high and exalted.
Thank you, Lord, your steadfast love endures forever.

Hebrews 4:16 (NIV) Let us therefore come boldly unto the throne of grace, that we may obtain mercy, and find grace to help in time of need.

13
YOU DON'T HAVE TO BE PERFECT TO BE USED BY GOD

Therefore there is now no condemnation...

Romans 3:23-24 For all have sinned and fall short of the glory of God, and are justified by his grace as a gift, through the redemption that is in Christ Jesus.

Father, I am so thankful that you have shown me in your Word I don't have to be perfect to serve you. I know that there are no perfect people, but many times I ask *How can You use me?* How can You use me when you know everything about me? Then, I realize how amazing and loving you truly are. You don't call people because they are rich or successful. You don't call people because they are great orators or seem to be the most popular. You call people because you see their hearts and don't condemn them for their past. You give us examples throughout the Word of broken, poor and misguided people.

When I look at these examples I am encouraged. David was a man after your own heart, yet he was a murderer. Paul persecuted Christians and had them murdered until he met you. Moses had a stuttering speech problem. Abraham was old. Rahab was a prostitute. Jacob was a cheater. Jonah ran away from you. Martha was a worrier. Peter denied that he even knew you.

What powerful examples these men and women were. You used each of them for great things, despite their status or past. Even today, there are men and women around the world who have done mighty works in your name, yet they led "colorful" pasts. Some lost businesses, others had affairs, some committed murder, some were drug dealers, drug addicts, abusers, liars and cheaters. Then one day You saved them. They found you and when they did, you no longer saw their past but invaded their future. Now they call you Lord and Savior and you met them right where they were, no matter what they had done, you welcomed them into your Kingdom.

Father, I am thankful that you call us, then teach and equip us to do what's necessary to fulfill that call. Remind me daily that there is no condemnation to those who love you. *Romans 8:1 (NIV) Therefore, there is now no condemnation for those who are in Christ Jesus.*

When Satan (the enemy) throws my past up to me, remind me that he was defeated by the blood of Jesus and therefore I will walk fully in the call that you have placed within me. I will not let the enemy's voice be louder than your voice. Use me to make a difference!

In Jesus' name. Amen.

14

PERSISTENT IN MY PURSUIT OF GOD

But seek ye first the kingdom of God...

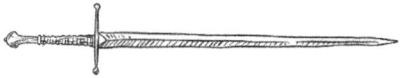

1 Peter 5:8-9 NIV (1984) Be self-controlled and alert. Your enemy the devil prowls around like a roaring lion looking for someone to devour. Resist him, standing firm in the faith, because you know that your brothers throughout the world are undergoing the same kind of sufferings.

Father, it is my desire to pursue and search your depths. Help me to be persistent in my faith and endeavors to go deeper in you. Don't let me get distracted by the day-to-day issues I face.

Everyday life screams loudly for me to be pulled from here to there. Everything seems critical at that moment, but most things are not. I realize this is a trick of the enemy to keep me from you. I know your Word says the enemy goes about like a roaring lion. Help me to recognize and resist the enemy, not falling for his tricks. I choose to not let his roar be louder than your voice. Help me to be sensitive to Holy Spirit so I will be persistent, standing in the faith and not be one the enemy devours. Your Word says in *Matthew 6:33 (KJV) But seek ye first the kingdom of God, and his righteousness; and all these things shall be added unto you.* My true desire, Lord, is to know you, to be persistent in my pursuit to follow you and seek Your Kingdom. What a great promise that if I seek you and your righteousness all these things will be added to me. I realize that seeking you is the greatest quest I can undertake, so I choose this day to be persistent in my pursuit of your depths.

In Jesus' name. Amen.

15

GOD IS MY PROBLEM SOLVER

I can do all this through him who gives...

Matthew 7:7-8 (NIV) says, "Ask and it will be given to you; seek and you will find; knock and the door will be opened to you. For everyone who asks receives; the one who seeks finds; and to the one who knocks, the door will be opened."

Father, I come before you today because I have a problem that seems too big for me to overcome.

I read your Word and I know that over and over it shows me you are my Problem Solver, but what I have been experiencing is overwhelming. Father, I need wisdom, knowledge and understanding on how to move forward. Right now, I feel paralyzed. I need to hear from you. I need direction.

A Word from the Lord to You

My Child, I hear your cry. I always hear your cry. My Word, that you have been holding in your hand and heart, has the answer to every question that you, the enemy or life's circumstances can throw at you.

First, understand that you can do all things through Christ who strengthens you. Phil. 4:13. Second, you must believe that no matter the outcome, I will make a way. Isaiah 43:15-16. Third, you must search the depths of my Word and listen for your solution. Prov. 4:20. Fourth, once you see the solution in my Word, you must act. You must be intentional to speak my Word over your problem. You must be intentional in binding any demonic strategies that are trying to attempt to keep you focused on your problem instead of me, Your Solution. You must loose all of heaven to invade your problem. My Word says in Matt. 16:19 I will give you the keys of the kingdom of heaven; whatever you bind on earth will be bound in heaven, and whatever you loose on earth will be loosed in heaven. These are not idle words that were spoken. Notice, I said these are the "keys to the Kingdom of Heaven." This is how you and I problem solve. This is an active life you have chosen in me. Serving me is not passive. You will always have "problems" to solve, but you will have victories to celebrate. Focus on the outcome my Word says you can have. Focus on me, your Problem Solver. Do not focus on your problem. I AM the Light into your darkness. When darkness starts to creep in, turn on the Light. Says your Lord.

Thank you, Lord, for that Word. It makes the scripture—talking about asking, seeking and knocking—clearer. Thank you for opening the door of my understanding. Thank you that I asked, I sought and I knocked and you answered. What a powerful God you are. Today I choose to look at you, my Problem Solver, rather than look at my problem.

In Jesus' name. Amen.

16

PRAYING AND UNDERSTANDING
YOUR PURPOSE

I cry out to God Most High...

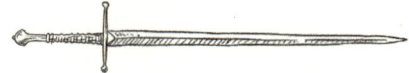

Psalm 57:2 (ESV) says, I cry out to God Most High, to God who fulfills his purpose for me.

Ephesians 2:10 (ESV) For we are His workmanship, created in Christ Jesus for good works, which God prepared beforehand that we should walk in them. (This verse clearly shows you that you were intentionally made for a purpose. You were never an accident.)

1 Peter 2:9 (NIV) But you are a chosen people, a royal priesthood, a holy nation, God's special possession, that you may declare the praises of him who called you out of darkness into his wonderful light.

Jeremiah 29:11 (NIV) "For I know the plans I have for you," declares the LORD, "plans to prosper you and not to harm you, plans to give you hope and a future."

Proverbs 19:21 (NIV) Many are the plans in a person's heart, but it is the LORD's purpose that prevails.

Romans 8:28 (NIV) And we know that in all things God works for the good of those who love him, who have been called according to his purpose.

Ephesians 2:10 (NIV) For we are God's handiwork, created in Christ Jesus to do good works, which God prepared in advance for us to do.

A Word from the Lord

My Child, My word says in Jer. 29:11 For I know the plans I have for you "plans to prosper you and not to harm you, plans to give you hope and a future." I see your desire to understand your purpose. I know that you want a hope and a future, that is why I promised them. You feel as if you are faltering and adrift in life like a ship without a sail. Be confident that I have a purpose for you. You were created with purpose, therefore, you have a purpose. Your main purpose is to love and worship me. To live a life that will draw others unto me. In every area of your life, you need to walk in a manner that piques the curiosity of others and causes them to want to know what you know. That causes them to see me in you, so strongly, they desire Me, as greatly as you do. Then your purpose is to serve me where you are planted. Whether you are a father or a mother, a daughter or a son, a grandparent or friend. Whether you are a business owner, a church leader or an employee. In other words, no matter where you find yourself on any given day, you are to show people my love through you. As you walk in obedience and love, you will see your life transform into something beautiful, something complete, something so fulfilling, that even on days that seem to be your toughest, you see a way through because you understand you have this purpose to love and see the world through my eyes. As you do this, your hope and your future will clearly come into focus. Says your Lord.

Father, thank you for that Word. *Psalm 57:2 says, I cry out to God Most High, to God who fulfills his purpose for me.* Please help me to walk in the fulness of my purpose, to be cognizant that my first purposeful act every day is to love and worship you, then let that love flow from you, through me, to others. Give me revelation knowledge of my hope and future, as it pertains to my work, my family, my friends and my church. Keep me on the path you created for me. Do not let me deviate from my purpose. I thank you for where you have planted me, even if I am only here for a short season. I thank you that no matter where I am, you are right there with me, teaching me, leading me and guiding me, so that my life honors you and helps others to do the same.

In Jesus' name. Amen.

17
STAY ENGAGED, FIGHT!

Fight the good fight of faith...

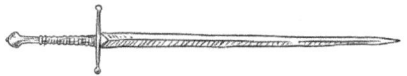

*2 Cor. 2:14 (KJV) Now thanks be unto God, **which always causes us to triumph** in Christ.*

A Word from the Lord

My Child, I hear you saying that you are weary, I hear you saying you've done everything you know to do, but breakthrough has not come. I am telling you today to not give up the fight. Stay engaged with me. Just because you do not get an answer the first day you pray, or the first month pray and yes, even the first year that you pray, doesn't mean that victory is not just around the corner. YOU MUST STAY ENGAGED WITH ME. I am moving on your behalf. I am creating the tapestry of your life. You cannot see the entire finished product, but I do. Trust in Me for your victory. Stay engaged. Keep praying, keep believing, keep standing, keep speaking my Word. Too many times you give up just before breakthrough. I AM YOUR GOD OF VICTORIES! I AM YOUR GOD OF BREAKTHROUGH! The enemy is the god of failures. Sometimes you must fight. Sometimes you must go into your prayer closet, your war room and fight. You will not go through life without trials and tribula-

tion, BUT, I have promised abundant life! To achieve the victories you must engage, use your Sword (MY Word) and FIGHT! DO NOT GIVE UP! DO NOT GIVE UP! DO NOT GIVE UP!

John 10:10 (KJV) The thief cometh not, but for to steal, and to kill, and to destroy: I am come that they might have life, and that they might have it more abundantly.

Daniel 10:12-14 (MSG) Relax, Daniel, he continued, don't be afraid. From the moment you decided to humble yourself to receive understanding, your prayer was heard, and I set out to come to you, but I was waylaid by the angel-prince of the kingdom of Persia and was delayed for a good three weeks. But then Michael, one of the chief angel-princes, intervened to help me.

1 Sam. 12:16 (KJV) Now therefore stand and see this great thing, which the Lord will do before your eyes.

Eph. 6:14 (KJV) Stand therefore, having your loins girt about with truth, and having on the breastplate of righteousness;

1 Tim. 6:12 (KJV) Fight the good fight of faith, lay hold on eternal life, whereunto thou art also called, and hast professed a good profession before many witnesses.

18
PRAYING THROUGH ANXIETY

You, LORD are with me...

Phil. 4:6-7 (NIV) Do not be anxious about anything, but in every situation, by prayer and petition, with thanksgiving, present your requests to God. And the peace of God, which transcends all understanding, will guard your hearts and your minds in Christ Jesus.

Father, today I am anxious about my life and especially the things that seem to be out of my control. I know your Word tells me over and over not to worry because you have me right in the palm of your hand. But today the enemy's voice is loud. I am thankful I have your Word that can drown out the enemy's voice. I choose to speak your Word, so it gets it into my heart and mind. Pushing the thoughts of doubt, anxiety and fear far from me. As I speak these Words today let Holy Spirit bring them alive in me knowing that you are my only lifeline, agreeing with your word that says in *John 14:16 (AMP) And I will ask You, and You will give me another Helper (Comforter, Advocate, Intercessor—Counselor, Strengthener, Standby), to be with me forever.*

I speak these scriptures today:

Psalm 94:15 (NIV) When anxiety is great within me, your consolation brings me joy.

Psalm 55:22 (NIV) I will cast my cares on you Lord and you will sustain me; You will never let the righteous be shaken.

Matt. 6:34 (NIV) Therefore I will not worry about tomorrow, for tomorrow will worry about itself. Each day has enough trouble of its own.

Romans 8:28 (NIV) And I know that in all things You work for the good of those who love you, who have been called according to your purpose.

John 14:27 (NIV) Peace You leave with me; Your peace You give me. You do not give to me as the world gives. I will not let my heart be troubled and I will not be afraid.

Psalm 55:22 (NIV) I will cast my cares on You, Lord, and you will sustain me; You will never let the righteous be shaken.

Isaiah 41:10 (NIV) So I will not fear, for You are with me; I will not be dismayed, for You are my God. You will strengthen me and help me; You will uphold me with Your righteous right hand.

Joshua 1:9 (NIV) You have commanded me. Be strong and courageous. Do not be afraid; do not be discouraged, for You my Lord my God will be with me wherever I go.

Psalm 119:6 (GW) You Lord are with me; I will not be afraid. What can mere mortals do to me?

Thank you, Lord, your Word is now in me, speaking louder than the enemy's words. Thank you, Lord, that I have the peace that passes all understanding. Thank you, that the enemy's strategies of fear and anxiety have failed because of your Word. I have chosen to put your Word in my heart, and I now know that I can overcome any fear and anxiety because greater are you that is in me than he that is in the world.

In Jesus' name. Amen.

1 John 4:4 (NIV) You, dear children, are from God and have overcome them, because the one who is in you is greater than the one who is in the world.

PRAISE MOMENT #3

Hebrews 13:15 (ASV) Through him then let us continually offer up a sacrifice of praise to God, that is, the fruit of lips that acknowledge his name.

1 Chronicles 29:13 (ESV) And now we thank you, Our God, and praise your glorious name.

Lord, I praise you. I glorify you; I magnify your name.
You are worthy of all my praise.
You are worthy to be exalted above everything.
I praise you for your unbreakable covenant.
I praise you for your unconditional love.
I praise you for your faithfulness.
You indeed are worthy. Praise your Holy name.

19

PRAYING FOR PEACE IN THE MIDDLE OF GREAT GRIEF

May I thirst for you even as the tears...

1 Peter 5:7 (ESV) Casting all your anxieties on him, because he cares for you.

Psalm 34:18 (ESV) The Lord is near to the brokenhearted and saves the crushed in spirit.

Matthew 11:28-30 (ESV) Come to me, all who labor and are heavy laden, and I will give you rest.

Psalm 42:1 (CSB) As a deer longs for flowing streams, so I long for you, God.

Father, today I cry out in great sorrow. I almost can't breathe. This heaviness I feel is almost greater than I can bear. Your Word says that you are near to the brokenhearted and you save a crushed spirit. Well Lord, I am brokenhearted and crushed today. My tears won't stop. I have never felt anything like this before. I am crippled with grief. Please fill me with your comfort and peace and help get me to the other side of this.

A Word from the Lord

My child, I understand your grief. I am right here with you. I am holding you. I am wiping away your tears. As you look to me, know that Jesus is and was despised and rejected of men; He was a man of sorrows, and acquainted with grief. I understand how heart-wrenching this is for you and the others around you. Enter into my presence, for my wrap-around arms are here to comfort you, I am here to wipe away your tears and my love is more than enough, even if at this very moment you don't' feel like it. I will never leave you, though you feel like I am a million miles away, but my child, I am here, holding tight to you. I will turn your ashes to beauty.

Father, help me to remember your Words. Help me to draw strength from reading your Word and praying. Help me to daily cast this burden of grief onto you because it is way too heavy for me to carry on my own. I need you! I am asking that I feel the Comforter (Holy Spirit) active in my life. That I feel peace and strength in this time of breathlessness. Let me feel your arms wrapped around me. Let me hear your whispers in my ear telling me everything will be ok and that I will not always feel like my world is ending. Thank you, Lord, that I can have confidence that you are right here with me now and in every minute of my life.

In Jesus' name. 𝔄𝔪𝔢𝔫.

20

DO NOT DOUBT MY WORD

These things I have spoken unto you...

James 1:5-7 (NIV) If any of you lacks wisdom, you should ask God, who gives generously to all without finding fault, and it will be given to you. But when you ask, you must believe and not doubt, because the one who doubts is like a wave of the sea, blown and tossed by the wind.

Father, it is my sincere desire not to be blown and tossed by the wind due to doubt. Today, I am facing several things that, on the surface, look bad or impossible to overcome. I know what your Word says. I know I'm not supposed to doubt, however, today I'm not doing well. I need your Word to come alive in me. I need to build up my confidence that all things are possible with you. Give me wisdom, knowledge and understanding to walk through this to victory.

A Word from God

My child, you have all the tools you need to overcome this situation. You have all of heaven backing you. My Word is specific. I have instructed you on the weapons you are to use to be an overcomer. You must say what my Word says. My Word is your sword. It is the sword of the Spirit. It is your battle weapon. Why would you go to battle without bringing and using your weapon. My Word says that you are more than a conqueror. My Word says that you can do all things through Christ Jesus who strengthens you. My Word says that NO weapon formed against you shall prosper. My Word says that every tongue that rises up against you shall fail. My Word says that greater am I that is in you than he who is in the world. My Word says that your enemy is defeated by the blood of the Lamb and the word of your testimony. Did you hear that? THE WORD OF YOUR TESTIMONY. You are to speak my Word (which is your testimony) to your problems and to your enemies. This is how you fight your battles. Use the Sword of the Spirit, MY WORD!! Speak boldly and loudly. Do not let the enemy tell you this is stupid or embarrassing. The Sword of the Spirit Works. You must wield your sword every time you are up against anything.
Use My Word...

Rev. 12:11 (KJV) And they overcame him by the blood of the Lamb, and by the word of their testimony;

Romans 8:37 (KJV) Nay, in all these things we are more than conquerors through Him that loved us.

Phil. 4:13 (KJV) I can do all things through Christ who strengthens me.

John 16:33 (KJV) These things I have spoken unto you, that in me ye might have peace. In the world ye shall have tribulation: but be of good cheer; I have overcome the world.

1 John 4:4 (KJV) Ye are of God, little children, and have overcome them: because greater is he that is in you, than he that is in the world.

Isaiah 54:17 (NAB) Every weapon formed against you will fail, and you will condemn every tongue that rises up to judge you. Now Go to battle, fully armed. Do not set idly by and let life toss you to and fro. For I have given you everything you need. Says your Lord.

2 Peter 1:3-4 (NIV) His divine power has given us everything we need for a godly life through our knowledge of him who called us by his own glory and goodness. Through these he has given us his very great and precious promises, so that through them you may participate in the divine nature, having escaped the corruption in the world caused by evil desires.

21
DESIRING THE DEPTHS OF GOD

He only is my Rock and my Salvation...

Psalm 42:7 (ISV) Deep waters call out to what is deeper still; at the roar of your waterfalls all your breakers and your waves swirled over me.

Father, today I come to you desiring more of you. There is a scripture, *Psalm 42:4, that says, deep calls to deep.* I desire to go deeper in you Lord, to know you more fully and completely. I have a passion to know your heartbeat. I desire to be intimate with you, my innermost being is crying out to you today. Help me dive deep in you Lord, to the depths of who you are. Open your Word, let it jump off the pages with revelation. Let your Word take root and produce fruit within me to honor you and to help others. Help me to be sensitive to Holy Spirit revealing your heart and allowing Him to pray through me.

Let my heartbeat become one with yours today. Beating in a rhythm with yours that glorifies you.

Let me see and demonstrate your love for others. Help me see the depth of your compassion, the deepness of your forgiveness and mercy. Father, how glorious you are. Let me never take you for granted. Let me always be cognizant of your presence. Though the world around me might be crumbling, remind me that you are my Rock and my Salvation, my fortress and my God in whom I trust. *Psalm 62:6 (AMPC) He only is my Rock and my Salvation; He is my Defense and my Fortress, I shall not be moved.* Thank you, Father, that I shall not be moved by what I see, but I will be moved by you, the God I serve.

Thank you, that your loving kindness (covenant love) is greater than I can ever fathom. Reach deep within me to show me the deep within you.

In Jesus' name. Amen.

22

PRAY FOR THE DREAMS OF YOUR HEART TO COME TO PASS

... and he shall give thee the desires of thine heart.

Father, I thank you for your Word. I thank you LORD that you created me in your image and after your likeness. Father, you had a dream that caused a world to come into existence, a dream that caused mankind to be created. You spoke your vision for the future into existence. *Genesis 1:27 (NIV) So God created mankind in his own image, in the image of God he created them; male and female he created them.*

So, since I am created in your image I choose to believe that this pattern is how I am to create/speak to the desires that you put in my heart. LORD, you gave me a gift, something that I do really well, something that is my heart's desire. One of my desires is to use this gift to glorify you, to make a difference, to show people your love and desires for their success. My dream is to _____ . (fill in the blank with your dream)

I know this dream is from you. I know that the enemy has tried at every turn to stop my dream from coming to pass. But I speak your Word over my dream right now... *James 1:17 (NIV) Every good and perfect gift is from above, coming down from the Father of the heavenly lights, who does not change like shifting shadows.*

My dream will ultimately help many, it will help me, my family and many others. Therefore, I bind Satan and all his demons and cohorts from stopping my dream from coming to fruition. Your word says in *Psalm 37:4 (KJ21) Delight thyself also in the LORD, and he shall give thee the desires of thine heart.*

In *Luke 12:34 (KJV)* it says, *For where your treasure is, there will your heart be also.* My heart is to glorify you through this dream. So, I take a stand against the enemy. I bind his strategies to hold my dream back and I loose heaven to come to my rescue. My dream is not dead. I speak resurrection to my dream because it is a God dream. I speak to myself and tell my dream it's time to be resurrected.

Prophetic Word from God Concerning Dreams:

God said it's time to dream again.
Time for old Dreams to be reignited. Time for new dreams to be birthed.
It doesn't matter how old you or your dreams are.
It doesn't matter how young or new your dream is.
IT IS TIME TO DREAM AGAIN!
The enemy has been successful using demonic strategies that have delayed dreams that you
have had for years and even decades.
The enemy's reign of success is OVER. I am destroying his strategies; I am thwarting his plans.
He shall no longer prevail over you.
DID YOU HEAR ME?
THE ENEMY SHALL NO LONGER STOP YOUR DREAMS FROM BEING MANIFESTED.
You have a part to play in ensuring the manifestation of your Dreams.
Speak resurrection to them.

Tell them to come forth.
Speak my word over them.
Rehearse them in your spirit, WRITE THEM DOWN
and say with your mouth what you see.
Just as I spoke to Lazarus to come forth.
You speak loudly and boldly with great faith for your
dreams to come forth.
Many of my children have multiple dreams.
Call them ALL forth...call them ALL forth...call them
ALL forth!
Do not say that it has been too long, do not let others
tell you that
it is impossible.
Have I not said that ALL THINGS ARE POSSIBLE
WITH ME!
THIS IS NOT A REQUEST FOR YOU TO TAKE
LIGHTLY.
THIS IS NOT A REQUEST TO MAKE YOU FEEL
GOOD.
THIS IS A CALL TO ACTION...ALL OF HEAVEN IS
POISED
FOR YOU TO START RESURRECTING YOUR
Prophetic Word!

23
THE EXTRAVAGANCE OF GOD

I can do all things through Christ...

Ephesians 3:20 (TPT) *Never doubt God's mighty power to work in you. He will achieve infinitely more than your greatest request, your most unbelievable dream, and exceed your wildest imagination! He will outdo them all, for his miraculous power constantly energizes you.*

Father, what a marvelous promise. Thank you that you are an extravagant God. Thank you that you lavish your love upon me doing mighty miracles. Thank you for breathing your breath of life into my dreams, seeing that they are fulfilled. Thank you, LORD, that I am not limited to my own knowledge but that all things are possible because I am connected to you, the Living God, the God of more than enough, the God who hears me when I call out to you. The thought of it causes me to weep in adoration for you. It causes me to sing your praises and worship you.

What an honor to worship the GREAT I AM. *Exodus 3:14 (KJV) And God said unto Moses, I AM THAT I AM: and he said, Thus shalt thou say unto the children of Israel, I AM hath sent me unto you.*

What an honor to worship Jesus, my Savior. It's almost unfathomable, your extravagant love. You allowed your son to die on the cross because your love is so extravagant. You forgive me of anything that I might have done or will do because of this love. I can come to you at any time and ask for forgiveness because of this love. I can bring any problem to you because of this love. I can do all things through Christ Jesus because of this love.

Philippians 4:13 (KJV) I can do all things through Christ which strengtheneth me.

Help me LORD to show others even just a glimpse of your love. Help me to show my family, my friends, my co-workers and anyone that crosses my path, this great love of Yours.

This great love of Yours!

24

SHOW ME THAT YOU ARE IN THE DETAILS OF MY LIFE

I sought the LORD, and he answered me...

Father, I come to you today needing you in every detail of my life. I need to understand that you care about all aspects of my life. Your Word says in *Psalm 37:23-25 (NLT) The LORD directs the steps of the godly. He delights in every detail of their lives. Though they stumble, they will never fall, for the LORD holds them by the hand.*

Thank you for directing my steps and holding my hand at every point in my life, even if there are naysayers that tell me differently. I choose to hear your voice and read Your Word that states emphatically that you care about me and help me with anything, big or small. In fact, there is nothing too small for you. In *Luke 12:6-7 (NIV)* Your Word says, *Are not five sparrows sold for two pennies? Yet not one of them is forgotten by God. Indeed, the very hairs of your head are all numbered. Don't be afraid; you are worth more than many sparrows.* Hebrews 4:16 *(NIV)* says, *Let us then approach God's throne of grace with confidence, so that we may receive mercy and find grace to help us in our time of need. 1 John 3:1 (NIV) says, How great is the love the Father has lavished on us, that we should be called children of God!*

Father I am your child and just like parents take care of the details in their children's lives, You take care of me. The picture you paint in Psalms of you holding my hand, leading me through life is glorious.

These scriptures show absolutely that you are in the details. Not only are you concerned, but we can come boldly, bringing anything to you, having confidence that you hear us in our time of need.

Your Word says that you hear our cries, and you deliver us out of ALL of our distresses.

Psalm 34:4 (NIV) I sought the LORD, and he answered me; he delivered me from all my fears.

Many people think you are only concerned with the big things we face, but this shows that You are concerned with everything we face, big or small.

Thank you for showing me that Your love for me is why You are into the details of my life.

John 15:13 (NIV) Greater love has no one than this: to lay down one's life for one's friends.

Father your love is great, so unending, so spectacular, that you sent your Son Jesus, to die a horrific death on the cross, so I might live an abundant life. The only way for me to live an abundant life is for you to be in the details. I decree that you are in the details of my life, and I allow you to be in those details. I choose to acknowledge you in everything.

In Jesus' name. 𝔄𝔪𝔢𝔫.

PRAISE MOMENT #4

Psalm 100:4 (NKJV) Enter into His gates with thanksgiving, and into His courts with praise: be thankful unto Him and bless His name.

Father, thank you that I can enter into your gates with thanksgiving and your courts with praise.
I choose to do that now.
How amazing and wonderful it is to enter into your presence, giving you thanks for all my blessings.
I praise you for your goodness, your grace and your mercy.
I praise you for loving me even when I feel unlovable.
Today, I give you melodies of praise because You are my amazing Jesus, my Lord and my Savior.

25

PRAYER CONCERNING WEARINESS

Cast your cares on the Lord, and ...

*Daniel 7:25 (KJV) And he shall speak great words against the most High, **and shall wear out the saints of the most High**, and think to change times and laws: and they shall be given into his hand until a time and times and the dividing of time.*

Gal. 6:9 (NIV) Let us not become weary in doing good, for at the proper time we will reap a harvest if we do not give up.

Isaiah 40:28-30 (NIV) Do you not know? Have you not heard? The Lord is the everlasting God, the Creator of the ends of the earth. He will not grow tired or weary and his understanding no one can fathom. He gives strength to the weary and increases the power of the weak. Even youths grow tired and weary, and young men stumble and fall;

Matthew 11:28-30 (NIV) "Come to me, all you who are weary and burdened, and I will give you rest. Take my yoke upon you and learn from me, for I am gentle and humble in heart, and you will find rest for your souls. For my yoke is easy and my burden is light."

Hebrews 12:3 (NIV) Consider him who endured such opposition from sinners, so that you will not grow weary and lose heart.

Psalm 55:22 (NIV) Cast your cares on the Lord, and he will sustain you; he will never let the righteous be shaken.

Jeremiah 31:25 (NIV) I will refresh the weary and satisfy the faint.

Mark 4:16-17 (AMP) In a similar way these [in the second group] are the ones on whom seed was sown on rocky ground, who, when they hear the word, immediately receive it with joy [but accept it only superficially]; and they have no real root in themselves, so they endure only for a little while; then, when trouble or persecution comes because of the word, immediately they [are offended and displeased at being associated with Me and] stumble and fall away.

Father, today I come to you because I am extremely weary. I feel as if I'm being pulled in a thousand directions. Everyone and everything needs my attention. I know your Word says not to grow weary in well doing for at the proper time things will happen, but the pressure is smothering. Your Word says that your strength gives me rest. Teach me how to draw on your strength today, Lord, because I have none left. I feel like crawling in a hole and never coming out. Please help!

A Word from God

My Child, first, know that I love you. Second, know that I am right here with you. Third, know that I will get you through to the other side. My Word will sustain you; my Word will give you comfort. My Word will give you direction. My Word will energize you to continue. MY WORD IS YOUR WEARINESS BREAKER. The enemy will try to wear you out, so come out of your hole and listen to Me. There will always be people and things that want your time and attention, this will never change. But what can change is how you handle things, especially when you feel attacked on every side. Never forget that I AM MY WORD! So, when you read and speak My Word you are engaging me. Remember, My Word never returns void. My Word is the antidote to your problems. You cannot live apart from My Word. Another way of stating it would be that you cannot live without Me. While I know your burdens are heavy and the depths of them seem insurmountable, but engaging Me, by speaking My Word to your weariness, is the answer. The enemy will tell you that you have no way out, he will tell you that speaking My Word is foolish. IT IS NOT FOOLISH. IT IS YOUR WAY OUT! So, keep at the forefront of your mind that your help never leaves you, your help is waiting with open arms, your help is one acknowledgement away. Call out to Me, read and speak My Word and you will begin to feel your burdens lighten.

Speak these verses over yourself:

Thank you, Lord, that you give strength to the weary and increase the power of the weak. *Isaiah 40:29 (NIV)* Therefore, I have strength and power to overcome this feeling of heaviness.

Thank you, Lord, that I cast my cares on You, and you will sustain me; you will never let the righteous be shaken. *Psalm 55:22 (NIV)* I cast my cares on you today, knowing you will sustain me and never let me be shaken.

I will refresh the weary and satisfy the faint. Jeremiah 31:25 (NIV) Thank you, Lord, that you are refreshing me and causing me not to faint.

Let us not become weary in doing good, for at the proper time we will reap a harvest if we do not give up. Gal. 6:9 (NIV)
Lord, I know that If I rely on you and don't give up, I will not grow weary in well doing and in the proper time I will reap a harvest.

Father, I choose to walk by faith and not by sight! I choose to focus on how big you are. You are far bigger than anything—problem or feeling—I face. Thank you that your Word is my antidote.

In Jesus' name. Amen.

26

GOD IS MY VICTOR

No weapon formed against you shall prosper...

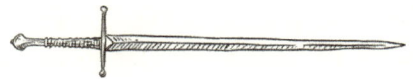

Father, thank you for being my Victor. In your Word one of your names is Jehovah Nissi—The Lord My Banner of Victory. *Exodus 17:15 (NLT)*

Because you are my victor, I come to you today needing victory over _____. In *Deut. 20:4 (NIV) For the Lord your God is he who goes with you to fight for you against your enemies, to give you the victory.*

You tell me you go with me to fight against my enemies, and you give me victory. Father, I need victory today. The enemy has been fighting against me. I am facing challenges that I never imagined that I would face. I know that when I face challenges, if I turn toward you, that you hear my cries and deliver me out all my troubles. *Psalm 24:17* says that when the righteous cry for help that You hear and deliver them from all their troubles. Give me perseverance so I can walk through this situation until I achieve victory through You. I know that these challenges can be conquered with you and through you!

I need deliverance, Lord. I need wisdom, knowledge and understanding today to know how to conquer and be victorious over this situation. Your Word in *Romans 8:37* also says that I am more than a conqueror. So, I choose this day to walk in the confidence that your Word operates perfectly in my life. I decree that I am more than a conqueror. I decree that I do Walk in Victory because you are my banner of Victory, I decree that when I cry out to you, you hear my prayers and deliver me.

I thank you, Father, that *Isaiah 54:17(NKJV)* states that no weapon formed against me shall prosper and every tongue that shall rise against me in judgment you shall condemn.

I refuse to accept defeat, because greater are you that is in me than he that is in the world.

In Jesus' name. Amen.

27

PRAY FOR UNDERSTANDING THAT GOD PURSUES YOU

For thus says the Lord God:

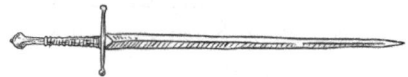

Genesis 3:9 (NIV) But the LORD God called to the man, "Where are you?"

Thank you, Father, that all throughout your Word, you pursue your people. You never leave us nor forsake us. *Hebrews 13:5 (ESV) Keep your life free from love of money, and be content with what you have, for he has said, "I will never leave you nor forsake you."*

Your Word says in *Ezekiel 34:11 (ESV) For thus says the Lord GOD: Behold, I, I myself will search for my sheep and will seek them out.* How powerful is that scripture verse Lord! You yourself will seek me out! You pursued Adam and Eve after they had sinned in the garden. Please remind me that if I sin against you, I can run toward you and not away from you because you are pursuing me. You also pursued Hagar when she ran away. She was mistreated by Sarai (Sarah). Father help me to not run away from you when I am mistreated by people. Help me to see you pursuing me no matter what state I am in.

In *1 Kings 19:1-9* tells the story of Elijah running from Jezebel. Elijah had killed all the prophets and Jezebel asked her gods to kill Elijah. He was so distraught that he ran away in fear for his life. Then Elijah prayed that he might die. He told the Lord that he had had enough. But God pursued Elijah and sent angels to provide food and water so that he would have strength to continue his journey, because God was not through with him. Thank you, Father, you don't give up on me, even if I give up. Remind me you are never done using me as long as I am living on this earth.

Finally, Lord, thank you for the example of Paul on the road to Damascus. Paul had done horrific things to the Jewish people, but that did not stop you from pursuing him and catching him on the Damascus Road. Thank you, Lord, for this example. Help me to understand and remember that no matter how far I get from you, you are right here, in fierce pursuit of me and if I go astray, YOU will catch me.

In Jesus' name. Amen.

Other Scripture References to look up:

Psalm 23:6 • Ezekiel 34:11 • Romans 8:34 • Luke 15:1-4

This prayer is for anyone who has, or desires to have, a business.

28

PRAYER FOR YOUR BUSINESS AS A MINISTRY

But the Lord is faithful...

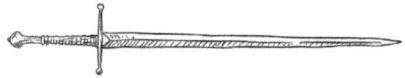

God's Word tells us that He gives us ideas and witty inventions. *Prov. 8:12 (KJV) I wisdom, dwell with prudence, and find out knowledge of witty inventions.* He doesn't just do that so we can support our families financially or support a certain lifestyle, He does this so we, as business owners, can make a difference to the people we have influence over every day. As a business owner we have a unique opportunity to show Christ's love through us, to our employees, our customers and our vendors. If you are a Christian and God has blessed you with a business, then it is God's will for you to steward your business and use it as a tool to further the Kingdom of God.

Father, I come to you today in a posture of thanksgiving, acknowledging that you have given me this business. You opened doors and gave me favor to be able to provide for my family. Help me to realize this business is to be used for a far greater purpose than just supporting my lifestyle. Give me wisdom, knowledge and understanding on how to use my business as a ministry to Glorify you and to bring people into the Kingdom.

Reveal to me what specifics I can do to be a light into a dark world. There is a unique opportunity, as a business owner, to demonstrate integrity, trust, honesty, and respect, according to how your Word defines them. *Proverbs 11:3 (NIV) The integrity of the upright guides them, but the unfaithful are destroyed by their duplicity.*

Prov. 21:3 (NIV) To do what is right and just is more acceptable to the LORD than sacrifice.

2 Cor. 8:21 (NIV) For we are taking pains to do what is right, not only in the eyes of the Lord but also in the eyes of man.

Father, sometimes it feels difficult to walk out and show my faith in the business world. Fear creeps in and I think, what if I don't get the contract or lose a customer because they don't believe as I do. Help me to remember that Greater are you that is in me than he that is in the world. *1 John 4:4 (KJV) Ye are of God, little children, and have overcome them: because greater is he that is in you, than he that is in the world.*

Help me to understand that taking a stand could lead to someone's salvation and that is far more valuable than my fear of losing a contract or sale. I thank you Lord that you have my back, and I can go forth boldly, operating my business as a ministry. I speak your word that says in Isaiah 54:17 "No weapon that is fashioned against me shall succeed, and I shall refute every tongue that rises against me in judgment. This is the heritage of the servants of the Lord and their vindication from me, declares the Lord."

2 Thess. 3:3 (ESV) But the Lord is faithful. He will establish you and guard you against the evil one.

Deut. 31:6 (ESV) Be strong and courageous. Do not fear or be in dread of them, for it is the Lord your God who goes with you. He will not leave you or forsake you.

Thank you, Lord, that I can with confidence, operate my business as a ministry. You said in *Mark 16:15-16 (NIV) "Go into all the world and preach the gospel to all creation. Whoever believes and is baptized will be saved, but whoever does not believe will be condemned."*

I decree that my business will preach the gospel to all creation.

In Jesus' name. Amen.

29
STANDING IN THE GAP

God is our refuge and strength...

Ezekiel 22:30 (KJV) And I sought for a man among them, that should make up the hedge, and stand in the gap before me for the land, that I should not destroy it: but I found none.

Father, today I come before you in prayer, not for myself, but for others. Your Word says in Ezekiel that you sought a man to stand in the gap but could not find one. Today, Lord, I choose to stand in the gap for my family, friends, extended family and co-workers. I will be the one that you can count on to stand in the gap. Today, I cover them with the Word of God. I speak, that you are their refuge, their very present help in the time of trouble. I pray that no weapon formed against them shall prosper. I pray every evil scheme of the enemy be thwarted. I pray that your angels keep them from dashing their foot against the stone. That you make a way for them when they feel there is no way. I speak over them, that greater are you that is in them than he that is in the world. Let them feel your very presence in time of trouble. Let them know that you are their rock, their refuge, the God in whom they trust. Let them feel your love surrounding them. Wrap your arms around them, comfort them, guide them and refresh them. Let them know that they can do all things through Christ who strengthens them. Let them know that nothing is impossible with you. Roar into their lives loudly so they have great assurance that you are on their side. Pour out your blessings on them this day. Fill them with wisdom, knowledge and understanding. Cause their bodies to line up with your word that says by the stripes of Jesus they are healed. Cause their jobs and their business to flourish and let them walk in your overwhelming great favor. Cover them with your mercy and grace, filling them with compassion for others. Let your love for them overflow from them to others. Cause them to have great victory, great vision, great love and the desire to dive into your depths.

In Jesus' name. Amen.

Psalm 46:1 (NIV) God is our refuge and strength, an ever-present help in trouble.

Isaiah 54:17 (KJV) No weapon that is formed against thee shall prosper; and every tongue that shall rise against thee in judgment thou shalt condemn. This is the heritage of the servants of the Lord, and their righteousness is of me, saith the Lord.

Psalm 33:10 (KJV) The Lord foils the plans of the nations; he thwarts the purposes of the people.

Psalm 91:11-12 (KJV) For he shall give his angels charge over thee, to keep thee in all thy ways. They shall bear thee up in their hands, lest thou dash thy foot against a stone.

Isaiah 43:15-16 (KJV) I am the Lord, your Holy One, the creator of Israel, your King. Thus saith the Lord, which maketh a way in the sea, and a path in the mighty waters.

1 John 4:4 (KJV) Ye are of God, little children, and have overcome them: because greater is he that is in you, than he that is in the world.

Phil. 4:13 (KJV) I can do all things through Christ which strengthens me.

Matt. 19:26 (NIV) Jesus looked at them and said, "With man this is impossible, but with God all things are possible."

Isaiah 53:5 (KJV) But he was wounded for our transgressions, he was bruised for our iniquities: the chastisement of our peace was upon him; and with his stripes we are healed.

Prov. 3:4 (KJV) So shalt thou find favor and good understanding in the sight of God and man.

30

PRAYER FOR UNDERSTANDING FAITH

But without faith it is impossible to...

Father, in the name of Jesus I make my request known to you today because your Word says in *Phil. 4:6-7 (KJV) be careful for nothing; but in everything by prayer and supplication with thanksgiving **let your requests be made known** unto God. And the peace of God, which passeth all understanding, shall keep your hearts and minds through Christ Jesus.*

My prayer today, Lord, is for me to understand how Faith works and operates in my life. I want to know your perspective on faith. I want to have clear discernment on how I need to walk by faith for every area of my life. *2 Cor. 5:7 (NKJV) For we walk by faith, not by sight.*

I speak your Words over myself today. I choose to get them deep within my spirit, so that walking by faith is a lifestyle and not a lifeline. The Word of God will be the first thing I think of when I am facing a problem. I will not lean to my own understanding or the world's understanding. Your Word says in *Proverbs 3:5, Trust in the LORD with all your heart and lean not on your own understanding.* Your Word is perfect. Acknowledging your Word keeps me on the path you have created for me. Because your Word is perfect, I will choose to speak your Word of faith.

Father, your Word says in *Prov. 4:20-23 (NIV) My son, pay attention to what I say; turn your ear to my words. Do not let them out of your sight, keep them within your heart; for they are life to those who find them and health to one's whole body, above all else, guard your heart, for everything you do flows from it.*

Therefore, because your Word is life and health, I choose to pay attention to your Word. I choose to Speak your Words about faith over me and my family.

Your Word says in *Hebrews 11:6* But without faith it is impossible to please you. That's why I pray this prayer. It is my desire to walk by faith and please you. In *Luke 5:20,* Jesus saw the faith of the friends of the man who needed healing when they lowered him through the roof to Jesus. Those friends had great faith. Help me to demonstrate that type of faith to my friends and family so that they can see you through me.

In Jesus' name. Amen.

PRAISE MOMENT #5

1 Thessalonians 5:16-18 (ESV) "Rejoice always, pray without ceasing, give thanks in all circumstances; for this is the will of God in Christ Jesus for you."

1 Corinthians 15:57 (ESV) "But thanks be to God, who gives us the victory through our Lord Jesus Christ."

Father, today I choose to go throughout my day with an attitude of thanksgiving.
When challenges arise*, I will look to you with praise and thanksgiving, because I know you have the answer and will see me through to victory.*

31

PRAYER FOR UNDERSTANDING OF HOW GREAT GOD'S LOVE IS FOR ME AND FOR OTHERS

But I say unto you, Love your enemies...

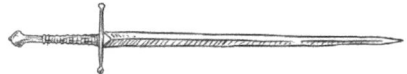

Eph. 3:17-19 (KJV) That Christ may dwell in your hearts by faith; that ye, being rooted and grounded in love, may be able to comprehend with all saints what is the breadth, and length, and depth, and height; And to know the love of Christ, which passeth knowledge, that ye might be filled with all the fulness of God.

Father, it is difficult to really understand the depth, breadth and width of your love. I come before you today asking for understanding concerning how much you love me, how much you love others, even when we seem to be unlovable by our standards and the world's.

First, I choose today to speak your Word concerning your love. I lay a foundation today, to allow for my understanding to be clear and felt within the inner most parts of my spirit, body, soul and heart. I make these scriptures personal by inserting my name, because I want your Word to come alive within me.

Insert your name in the blanks or anyone you know who needs to know they are loved.

John 3:16 (KJV) "For God so loved _____, (insert your name here) that he gave his only Son, that if _____ believes in him _____ should not perish but that _____ will have eternal life.

1 John 4:16 (KJV) So _____ comes to know and to believe the love that God has for _____. God is love, and whoever abides in love abides in God, and God abides in _____.

Romans 8:37-39 (NIV) No, in all these things we are more than conquerors through him who loved us. For I am convinced that neither death nor life, neither angels nor demons, neither the present nor the future, nor any powers, neither height nor depth, nor anything else in all creation, will be able to separate us from the love of God that is in Christ Jesus our Lord.

Father, help me to understand that your love is unstoppable. That you love every person you created, even those people who have so far in their lives rejected you. Give me a heart of love to pray for those that hurt me, those that hurt what you love. Your Word says in *Matt 5:44 But I say unto you, Love your enemies, bless them that curse you, do good to them that hate you, and pray for them which despitefully use you, and persecute you;*

Lord, let me see people as You see them.

Thank you that nothing can separate us from your love. Thank you that there is nothing too big for your forgiveness. Help me to experience your love through other people, help me to impart your love to others, even to the seemingly unlovable.

Jesus, you suffered so greatly because of your great love for us.

(Visualize a picture in your heart of Jesus taking stripes on his back, having a crown of thorns placed on his head, being nailed to the cross, then hanging on that cross in agonizing pain, all the while being ridiculed, mocked and laughed at. Only a few knew what he was really doing at that moment, and even they didn't truly understand the magnitude. Now understand that Jesus had YOU on his mind while he endured such horror.)

That is LOVE!
Now, Father, let my faith and love lead others to the cross. In Jesus' name. Amen.

32

PRAYERS CONCERNING CHANGE
BECAUSE GOD HAS A NEW DIRECTION FOR YOU TO GO

And whatever he does, he prospers...

Father, in Jesus name, I ask you to help me deal with change. Throughout my life change has been a constant, but often I do not handle change very well. I can be extremely slow to change or I can let change stop me. It is my desire to move forward in the things you have for me. I want to make a big impact in your Kingdom; to do the things I need to do to shift gears to go forward, but this has been difficult. Holy Spirit, I need your guidance to help me with the changes I am facing. I pray for confidence to know I can do all things through Christ who Strengthens me. *Phil. 3:13 (KJV) I can do all things through him who strengthens me.* Lord, I feel that you are tugging on my heart to change directions. Help me to stay focused on you and your calling. Keep me from staying in my comfort zone. It is easy to keep the status quo, but if you are asking me to move, then I agree with you and I will move. I will not allow fear, nor will I allow others' opinions to sway me from the direction you are leading me. I will not allow doubt to overtake me. I will not allow my age or status in life to stop me from accomplishing the call you have on my life. Even if I have never done what I feel you are speaking to me, I will still move forward with boldness and determination.

I choose to keep your Word in front me, helping me to rise to the challenge to change...

Psalm 1:3 (AMP) And he will be like a tree firmly planted [and fed] by streams of water, Which yields its fruit in its season; Its leaf does not wither; And in whatever he does, he prospers [and comes to maturity].

My mission is to walk with you and walk in the calling you have for me, and I shall prosper because I choose to plant myself firmly in the Word.

In Jesus' name. Amen.

33
PRAYER TO CONQUER FEAR

And ye are complete in him...

Father, in the name of Jesus, I am learning the importance of speaking your Word. So, I pray and speak your Word because the enemy has been trying to attack me and make me fearful. It doesn't matter whether I am dealing with worry, stress, anxiety or loss, your Word says in *2 Timothy 1:7 that you have not given me a spirit of fear but of power and love and a sound mind.* Your Word also states that no weapon formed against me shall prosper and that includes the weapon of fear. I refuse to allow the enemy to keep me walking in a place of fear. I choose a life free from the fear of the enemy. *2 Sam. 22:3* says you are *The God of my rock; in him will I trust: he is my shield, and the horn of my salvation, my high tower, and my refuge, my savior; thou savest me from violence.*

Father, you are my rock, my rescuer, my fortress. Who does the enemy think he is? He cannot intimidate me; he cannot make me fall; he cannot make me fail; he cannot make me give up. Jesus defeated the enemy and gave me complete victory. The Word says in *Col. 2:10 And ye are complete in him, which is the head of all principality and power.*

So, Lord, if I am complete in You and if I am in You (which I am) then there is no place for fear. Therefore, I choose the Words of Jesus, over the words and actions of Satan and his cohorts.

In Jesus' name. Amen.

34
PRAYER FOR YOUR SPOUSE

For I will restore health unto thee...

Father, in the name of Jesus, I pray that you help me be sensitive to the needs of my spouse. I pray that your perfect will be done in their life. I pray you show me what my spouse needs and how I can help with those needs. I ask for divine protection over them as they go about their day working, taking care of the home or on their job. I pray for clarity of mind and ask you fill them with wisdom, knowledge and understanding, concerning their calling from you. I ask that you give them the desires of their heart. (those deep, Godly dream desires) you placed within them. Fill them full of supernatural strength to accomplish life's tasks. Give them perfect focus to understand when to move and when to be still. Lord, you know everything about my spouse; their desires, their wants, their needs. Fill them according to your power. *Romans 15:13 (NIV) May the God of hope fill you with all joy and peace as you trust in him, so that you may overflow with hope by the power of the Holy Spirit.*

Lord, help me to always remember how much you love and value them. Help me to always value them as you do. No matter how hard some seasons of our life are, I choose to stand strong and support my spouse through all adversity.

I thank you that my spouse is a mighty warrior for you. Help them to stand strong no matter what comes their way. Help me to be strong when they are weak and my spouse to be strong when I am weak.

I pray they walk in divine health.

Jeremiah 30:17 (KJV) For I will restore health unto thee, and I will heal thee of thy wounds, saith the Lord;

I ask that they live a long life until they are satisfied.

Psalm 91:16 (NKJV) With long life will I satisfy him, and show him My salvation.

Keep our love and commitment strong.
In Jesus' name. Amen.

35

DEALING WITH PEOPLE WHO HURT YOU

You leave peace with me. Your peace you give me...

𝔉ather today I am coming before you with my heart broken. Someone I love deeply has hurt me. I don't understand how they could have done such a horrible thing. I trusted them. Now, they have broken that trust. I need to know how to act, how to respond, how to move forward.

A Word from God

My child, I knew you would cry out to me today. I feel your broken heart. Know that I am right here with you at this very moment. I see your tears; I feel your pain. My Word says that I am close to the broken hearted. Psalm 34:18 The LORD is close to the brokenhearted and saves those who are crushed in spirit. I realize that right now, in this very moment, your spirit is crushed. I need you to know that you can trust me. You can trust me to turn your mourning into dancing. You can trust me to wipe away your tears. You will get to the other side of this. 2 Cor. 4:8-9 (ESV) We are afflicted in every way, but not crushed;

perplexed, but not driven to despair; persecuted, but not forsaken; struck down, but not destroyed; I know you feel like you can't breathe at this moment, but you will overcome. I need you to speak my word of comfort and victory over yourself.
DO NOT KEEP REHEARSING THE HURT THAT WAS DONE TO YOU.
Speak these Words over yourself every time you start to dwell on the hurt.

1 Peter 5:7 (NIV) I cast all my anxiety on you because you care for me.

2 Cor. 5:7 (ESV) I walk by faith and not by sight or feelings.

2 Cor. 12:9 (NIV) "Your grace is sufficient for me, for Your power is made perfect in weakness."

Hebrews 13:5 (ESV) I know that you will never leave me nor forsake me.

Isaiah 41:10 (KJV) I will not fear, for I know you are with me; I will not be dismayed, for I know you are my God. I know you will strengthen me and help me; I know you uphold me with your righteous right hand.

Jer. 29:11 (NIV) I know the plans you have for me, plans to prosper me and not to harm me, plans to give me hope and a future.

John 14:27 (NIV) You leave peace with me. Your peace you give me. You do not give to me as the world gives. I will not let my heart be troubled and I will not be afraid.

Matt. 11:28 (NIV) I will come to you, because I am weary and burdened, and I know you will give me rest.

Prov. 3:5 (NIV) I will trust in you Lord with all my heart and lean not to my own understanding;

Psalm 147:3 (NIV) I know you heal the brokenhearted and bind up their wounds.

1 Cor. 15:57 (NIV) Now I give you thanks God, you give me the victory through my Lord Jesus Christ.

Romans 8:37 (NIV) And in all these things I am more than a conqueror through Him who loves me.

So today, Lord, I put the hurt and painful thoughts aside and choose to put on the full armor of God, so that I feel your power and love wrapped around me so I am able to stand my ground and after I have done everything I can still stand. *Ephesians 6:13 Therefore put on the full armor of God, so that when the day of evil comes, you may be able to stand your ground, and after you have done everything, to stand.*

In Jesus' name. Amen.

36

PRAYER FOR RESTORATION

But You will restore me to health and heal my wounds...

Father, I thank you that you are the God of restoration. *Isaiah 61:7 (NIV)* says... *Instead of your shame you will receive a double portion, and instead of disgrace you will rejoice in your inheritance.* And so you will inherit a double portion in your land, and everlasting joy will be yours. Lord, right now it seems impossible to think restoration could ever happen, much less that I feel everlasting joy. The journey has been difficult on good days. But you give me the example of Job, and how he lost almost everything, but because he never rejected you, You gave him complete restoration. *Job 42:10 (NIV) After Job had prayed for his friends, the LORD restored his fortunes and gave him twice as much as he had before. Job 42:12 (NIV) The LORD blessed the latter part of Job's life more than the former part.* Thank you, Lord, that you are not a respecter of persons and what you have done for one you will do for another. *Acts 10:34 (KJV) Then Peter opened his mouth, and said, Of a truth I perceive that God is no respecter of persons: Thank you that I can come boldly to you and make my request known.* So, I ask for complete restoration. I need restoration of my mind, so I don't dwell on the past. I need restoration for my body because it is weak. I need restoration in my family because there are relationships that need mending. I need restoration of my finances because others depend on me. But mostly Lord, I need restoration of my spirit because I have let darkness creep in. Restore your light in my spirit Lord so I can see clearly and expect your Word to restore my spirit.

Speak these out loud!

Isaiah 61:7 (NIV) Instead of shame I will receive a double portion, and instead of disgrace I will rejoice in my inheritance. And so I will inherit a double portion in your land, and everlasting joy will be mine.

Jeremiah 30:17 (NIV) "But You will restore me to health and heal my wounds," declares the LORD, "because I was called an outcast, Zion for whom no one cares."

2 Chron. 7:14 (NIV) If my people, who are called by my name, will humble themselves and pray and seek my face and turn from their wicked ways, then I will hear from heaven, and I will forgive their sin and will heal their land.

Job 42:10 (NIV) After Job had prayed for his friends, the LORD restored his fortunes and gave him twice as much as he had before.

Job 42:12 (NIV) The LORD blessed the latter part of Job's life more than the former part. Therefore, I can ask you Lord to bless the latter part of my life as well.

2 Kings 8:6 (NIV) The king asked the woman about it, and she told him. Then he assigned an official to her case and said to him, "Give back everything that belonged to her, including all the income from her land from the day she left the country until now."

Therefore, I can also ask and believe for total restoration.

1 Peter 5:10 (NIV) And the God of all grace, who called me to his eternal glory in Christ, after I have suffered a little while, will himself restore me and make me strong, firm and steadfast.

Psalm 51:12 (NIV) Restore to me the joy of your salvation and grant me a willing spirit, to sustain me.

Isaiah 61:7 (NIV) Instead of my shame I will receive a double portion, and instead of disgrace I will rejoice in my inheritance. And so I will inherit a double portion in my land, and everlasting joy will be mine.

Acts 3:21 (NIV) Heaven must receive him until the time comes for God to restore everything, as he promised long ago through his holy prophets.

Joel 2:25 (NIV) I will repay you for the years the locusts have eaten— the great locust and the young locust, the other locusts and the locust swarm— my great army that I sent among you. Thank you, Lord, that I will be repaid for the things that the enemy has stolen.

Ezekiel 22:30 (NASB) I searched for a man among them who would build up the wall and stand in the gap before Me for [the sake of] the land, that I would not destroy it, but I found no one [not even one].

Colossians 1:9 (NIV) For this reason, since the day we heard about you, we have not stopped praying for you. We continually ask God to fill you with the knowledge of his will through all the wisdom and understanding that the Spirit gives.

Matt. 5:44 (NIV) But I say unto you, Love your enemies, bless them that curse you, do good to them that hate you, and pray for them which despitefully use you, and persecute you;

1 Timothy 2:1 (KJV) I exhort therefore, that, first of all, supplications, prayers, intercessions, and giving of thanks, be made for all men;

1 Peter 3:15 (NLT) Instead, you must worship Christ as Lord of your life. And if someone asks about your hope as a believer, always be ready to explain it.

Hebrews 7:25 (NIV) Therefore he is able to save completely those who come to God through him, because he always lives to intercede for them.

Colossians 3:13 (NIV) Bear with each other and forgive one another if any of you has a grievance against someone. Forgive as the Lord forgave you.

Luke 6:28 (NIV) Bless those who curse you, pray for those who mistreat you.

Matt. 6:14 (NIV) For if you forgive other people when they sin against you, your heavenly Father will also forgive you.

Job 42:10 (NIV) After Job had prayed for his friends, the LORD restored his fortunes and gave him twice as much as he had before.

1 Thess. 5:17 (NIV)...pray continually

PRAISE MOMENT #6

Psalm 103:1-4 (NIV) Praise the LORD, my soul; all my inmost being, praise His holy name. Praise the LORD, my soul, and forget not all His benefits — who forgives all your sins and heals all your diseases, who redeems your life from the pit and crowns you with love and compassion.

Psalm 118:24 (ESV) This is the day that the Lord has made, I will rejoice and be glad in it.

1 Chronicles 16:34 (NIV) Give thanks to the Lord, for he is good; his love endures forever.

Psalm 28:7 ESV) The Lord is my strength and my shield; in him my heart trusts, and I am helped; my heart exults, and with my song I give thanks to him.

Thank you, Father, that you redeemed me from the pit, and you crown me with love and compassion.
I will rejoice and be glad because today is a day you have made.
I will give thanks to you today for you are good and your mercy endures forever. Hallelujah, thank you Jesus!

37

GOD IS CALLING YOU!

But how can people call on him for help if they've not...

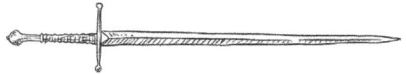

A Word from God

My child, today I want you to listen intently. I am calling you. I am calling you to be a light in a dark world. The hour is critical for you to accept this call. Many lives depend on you answering my call. Listen, Listen, Listen. Holy Spirit is talking to you. I have great plans for My kingdom, I have great plans for you. Do not think that you are inadequate to answer the call. I have given you all the tools you need to walk completely in Me.
Where are you planted? What are you doing today? Are you growing? Are you stagnant? Are you being blown by the winds of this world from here to there, without purpose? Take stock of where you are. Listen, Listen, Listen. I am calling you. Unplug your ears and hear! There is a world that is lost. My heart is calling you to help. The world needs My son, Jesus. Who will tell them? Will you answer the call? If you listen closely, you will not only hear my heartbeat, you will feel my love and compassion for the lost. I need you to tell them about My Son. I need you to show them His mighty works. I need them to experience signs and

wonders. I want to heal them. I want to deliver them. I want to set them free. But they must hear. How can they hear unless my children answer the call and tell them? Go into all the world was not an idle statement. It is part of your calling. Don't let the busyness of life get in the way. Don't let it keep you from your call. I need you, my child.

Now that you've heard, it's time to act. It's time to dig deep. Now, is not the time to be still. The world needs you. I need you. Don't wait until you have everything "in order". Today is the day of salvation. Spread it to the world. One person at a time. You don't have to be a great orator, you don't' have to be bold. I work within your personality. I made you. No matter who you are, no matter how bold or shy, no matter how popular or isolated you are, I AM CALLING YOU! Let Me show myself mighty in and through you... ANSWER THE CALL!

Romans 10:14 (TPT) But how can people call on him for help if they've not yet believed? And how can they believe in one they've not yet heard of? And how can they hear the message of life if there is no one there to proclaim it?

38

PRAYER FOR OUR NATION

Righteousness exalteth a nation: but sin...

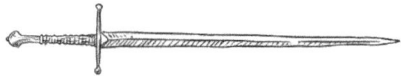

1 Tim 2:1-2 (KJV) I exhort therefore, that, first of all, supplications, prayers, intercessions, and giving of thanks, be made for all men; For kings, and for all that are in authority; that we may lead a quiet and peaceable life in all godliness and honesty.

Psalm 33:6-12 (KJV) By the word of the L<small>ORD</small> were the heavens made; and all the host of them by the breath of his mouth. He gathereth the waters of the sea together as an heap: he layeth up the depth in storehouses. Let all the earth fear the L<small>ORD</small>: let all the inhabitants of the world stand in awe of him. For he spake, and it was done; he commanded, and it stood fast. The L<small>ORD</small> bringeth the counsel of the heathen to nought: he maketh the devices of the people of none effect. The counsel of the L<small>ORD</small> standeth for ever, the thoughts of his heart to all generations. Blessed is the nation whose God is the L<small>ORD</small>; and the people whom he hath chosen for his own inheritance.

Proverbs 13:34 (KJV) Righteousness exalteth a nation: but sin is a reproach to any people.

Father, in the name of Jesus, I bring my nation before you. I ask that you move upon our nation so that truth, justice and righteousness prevail. Father, it is obvious that the enemy (Satan and his minions) have a demonic agenda to keep truth, justice and righteousness from prevailing in our land. There are people that the enemy is using to cause ungodly agendas to be propelled forward. Today I speak against those agendas. I speak against the demonic strategies that would try to take over our Nation. I speak against anything that would keep you from being the center and foundation of our nation. Your word says in *Ephesians 6:11 (KJV) Put on the whole armor of God, that ye may be able to stand against the wiles of the devil.* So, today I put on the armor of God and use the Sword of the Spirit (The WORD) to stand my ground and defeat these ungodly agendas.

Father, I speak in the name of Jesus that no weapon formed against my nation will prosper. I speak that every fiery dart of the enemy will be thwarted. That means any terrorist attempts, or other evil deeds that the enemies of my nation are trying to carry out shall be unsuccessful. Protect our leaders. Give them Godly wisdom, knowledge and understanding on how to govern this nation as you would have them govern. Let your power flow in this nation, causing peace, truth, justice and righteousness to prevail. 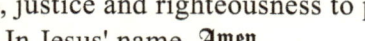 In Jesus' name. Amen.

39

PRAISE AND WORSHIP

The Lord your God is with you...

ather, how do I worship you? How do I enter into your presence? Every day I feel drawn to you, but I feel so inadequate to think that you want to hear from me. You have a chorus of angels that daily circle your throne crying Holy, Holy, Holy is the Lord God Almighty. What can my voice add to that?

A Word from the Lord

My Child, you were created to worship Me. That is the reason you feel so drawn to me. I desire to hear your praises; I desire to feel your love through worship and praise. Your praises create a symphony of voices in heaven that is majestic, awesome and powerful. The enemy might tell you that it is foolish, but it is not. He knows the power of worship. The enemy knows that strongholds can be broken through praise and worship. So, fight through the noise and begin to praise and worship me every day.

2 Chron. 20:22 (NKJV) Now when they began to sing and to praise, the Lord set ambushes against the people of Ammon, Moab, and Mount Seir, who had come against Judah; and they were defeated.

So, when you praise and worship Me, you are not just entering My presence to thank me, you are causing heaven to move on earth with the power of My victory. Never underestimate the impact of your praise and worship, for it is extremely powerful on many levels. It can move mountains; it can calm storms; it pulls Heaven into any situation you are experiencing. Don't ever forget that. So Praise Me, for I am singing over you!

Zeph. 3:17 (NIV) The Lord your God is with you, the Mighty Warrior who saves. He will take great delight in you; in his love he will no longer rebuke you but will rejoice over you with singing.

Come into my presence singing with joy! For what joy it should be to you, knowing I am your Creator. You are made to worship and praise me. Thank me for who I am and for all I've done. Be thankful for my plan of creation, salvation and redemption. Be thankful that Jesus suffered the cross for your victory. Be thankful for the power of my Word, for it is your offensive weapon against the enemy; it is your strength, your direction. Be thankful for Holy Spirit for He guides you in all your ways. Praise Me and worship me for My goodness, My grace, My mercy and My love. Praise me because I don't ever give up on you, I am continually pursuing you.
Praise and worship because I am your Creator, Savior and King!

Psalm 100:1-5 (NKJV) Make a joyful shout to the Lord, all you lands! Serve the Lord with gladness; Come before His presence with singing. Know that the Lord, He is God; It is He who has made us, and not we ourselves; We are His people and the sheep of His pasture. Enter into His gates with thanksgiving, And into His courts with praise. Be thankful to Him, and bless His name. For the Lord is good; His mercy is everlasting, And His truth endures to all generations.

40
ENGAGING HEAVEN
Rejoice always, pray continually...

Matt. 16:19 (NIV) I will give you the keys of the kingdom of heaven; whatever you bind on earth will be bound in heaven, and whatever you loose on earth will be loosed in heaven.

John 14:14 (NIV) You may ask me for anything in my name, and I will do it.

Mark 11:24 (NIV) Therefore I tell you, whatever you ask for in prayer, believe that you have received it, and it will be yours.

Father, I ask you today to help me to realize just how powerful prayer is. Show me that heaven is really standing at attention waiting on me to engage. Help me realize you need me and the rest of the church to pray. Remind me that prayer changes things in the spirit realm, **that prayer is my voice aligned with your Word causing victory to be manifested** in my life and the lives of those I am praying for. Thank you that your Word shows me prayer isn't something I do when things are going bad, but that prayer is a lifestyle. Your Word says in *Ephesians 6:18 (NIV) And pray in the Spirit on all occasions with all kinds of prayers and requests. With this in mind, be alert and always keep on praying for all the Lord's people. James 5:16 (NIV) Therefore confess your sins to each other and pray for each other so that you may be healed.* ***The prayer of a righteous person is powerful and effective.***

1 Thessalonians 5:16-18 (NIV) Rejoice always, pray continually, give thanks in all circumstances; for this is God's will for you in Christ Jesus.

Thank you, Lord, that these verses are clear. Prayer should be continual and active in my daily life. Remind me, Lord, to engage heaven throughout the day, speaking your Word over any situation or need that I, or those near me, face.

A Word from the Lord

My child, hearing you call out My name is one of the sweetest sounds I can hear. I so want to talk with you throughout your day. Just as you love hearing from those you love dearly, it is the same for me. Engaging with Me gives you strength, clarity, determination, focus and compassion. I am right here in every moment for you. Start tuning into my frequency during your day. The world has so many frequencies that vie for your attention, but I AM the one whom you need the most. Find my frequency as you start your day. I hear you saying, "but Lord I'm too busy throughout the day to stop and pray." I did not say Stop and Pray. I said, stay tuned into my frequency, so that you can engage Me instantly. Tune in before you start a meeting, before you get out of your car, before interacting with others. I am speaking always. Select a verse from My Word to think about daily. Then, as you go throughout your day, let Me remind you of that verse. Remember My word is a light unto your path. Let me illuminate your path each and every day. It's not a hard thing, it's a new habit you need to create. Be sensitive to Holy Spirit, he will keep you in the flow of my frequency, but you must want to be there.

Psalm 119:105 (NIV) Thy word is a lamp unto my feet, and a light unto my path.

41

PRAYING FOR GOD'S FAVOR

For by grace you have been saved through faith...

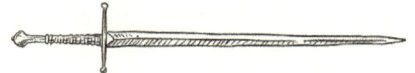

Father, today I am being thankful that throughout your Word, your desire is for me to walk in your favor. *Psalm 84:11(NIV) For the LORD God is a sun and shield; the LORD bestows favor and honor; no good thing does he withhold from those whose walk is blameless.* Your Word also says that you search the whole earth looking for someone to show yourself strong. *2 Chronicles 16:9 (KJV) For the eyes of the LORD run to and fro throughout the whole earth, to shew himself strong in the behalf of them whose heart is perfect toward him.* Father, I know that only through the blood of the Lamb am I blameless and perfect, because the blood cleanses me from all unrighteousness. I am so thankful for your plan of salvation and deliverance. Because of that plan, I now know that I can walk in the fullness of your favor.

Your Word says you bestow favor and honor. Lord, I have many goals I want to accomplish in my life, but I know these goals would be impossible without your favor. Most importantly Lord, I want my desires to line up with your will so I can boldly come to your throne asking for your grace, mercy and favor to overtake me and my family.

Hebrews 4:16 (KJV) Let us therefore come boldly unto the throne of grace, that we may obtain mercy, and find grace to help in time of need.

I ask, as you search the earth, your eyes stop upon me. I want to be a warrior for you Lord. I want to do mighty exploits for your kingdom. Father, I want your favor to help me lead others into your presence. I want your favor to help me help others to change their lives, by bringing them into your kingdom.

Psalm 90:17 (NKJV) Let the favor of the Lord our God be upon us, and establish the work of our hands upon us; yes, establish the work of our hands!

Father, let your favor move people, places, things and events in and out of my life to accomplish your perfect will for my life. I need you in every area, not so I can boast, but so I can show others how big the one and only Living God I serve truly is.

In Jesus' name. Amen.

Ephesians 2:8-10 (NKJV) For by grace you have been saved through faith, and that not of yourselves; it is the gift of God, not of works, lest anyone should boast. For we are His workmanship, created in Christ Jesus for good works, which God prepared beforehand that we should walk in them.

PRAISE MOMENT #7

Psalm 136 (NIV)

Give thanks to the Lord, for he is good. *His love endures forever.*
Give thanks to the God of gods. *His love endures forever.*
Give thanks to the Lord of lords: *His love endures forever.*
to him who alone does great wonders, *His love endures forever.*
who by his understanding made the heavens, *His love endures forever.*
who spread out the earth upon the waters, *His love endures forever.*
who made the great lights—*His love endures forever.*
the sun to govern the day, *His love endures forever.*
the moon and stars to govern the night; *His love endures forever.*
to him who struck down the firstborn of Egypt *His love endures forever.*
and brought Israel out from among them *His love endures forever.*
with a mighty hand and outstretched arm; *His love endures forever.*
to him who divided the Red Sea asunder *His love endures forever.*
and brought Israel through the midst of it, *His love endures forever.*
but swept Pharaoh and his army into the Red Sea; *His love endures forever.*
to him who led his people through the wilderness; *His love endures forever.*
to him who struck down great kings, *His love endures forever.*
and killed mighty kings—*His love endures forever.*
Sihon king of the Amorites *His love endures forever.*
and Og king of Bashan—*His love endures forever.*
and gave their land as an inheritance, *His love endures forever.*
an inheritance to his servant Israel. *His love endures forever.*
He remembered us in our low estate *His love endures forever.*
and freed us from our enemies. *His love endures forever.*
He gives food to every creature. *His love endures forever.*
Give thanks to the God of heaven. *His love endures forever.*

Father, you have given us so much to be thankful for.
Thank you that your love endures forever.
Thank you, Jesus, for the victory. Thank you, Holy Spirit, for revelation knowledge of the Word and for helping me to grow every day.
Hallelujah to the Lord Most High!

42

PRAYING FOR ISRAEL

For we do not wrestle against flesh and blood...

𝔉ather, today I pray for Israel. Your Word says in *Psalm 122:6 (NKJV) Pray for the peace of Jerusalem: "May they prosper who love you."* I love Jerusalem, Lord, and I pray for Jerusalem's peace today. It feels as if the entire world is against them. I know Israel is surrounded on every side by those who want its complete destruction, but I also know that Israel is the apple of your eye. *Zechariah 2:8 (NKJV) For thus says the Lord of hosts: "He sent Me after glory, to the nations which plunder you; for he who touches you touches the apple of His eye.* Father, I speak with the authority you have given me through the blood of Jesus, that no weapon formed against Israel will prosper. I speak that the principalities, powers and the rulers of darkness are of no affect at any scheme they have devised against Israel. I thank you Lord, that Israel is protected from the River to the Sea. Protect the people of Israel, Lord. Give them the strength to fight, to stand, and to believe that You will never let them down. Lord, I thank you that You will never leave them or forsake them, and they will always be victorious. Lord, confuse and confound their enemies. Let their enemies see all of heaven coming to Israel's rescue. Let the victories of Israel be a sign to the Nations that the one and only Living God is Israel's God. Let their victories also show the peoples of the earth that they need to worship the God of Abraham, Isaac and Jacob through Jesus, the Son. Let salvation be magnified through Israel's victories.

Ephesians 6:12 (NKJV) For we do not wrestle against flesh and blood, but against principalities, against powers, against the rulers of the darkness of this age, against spiritual hosts of wickedness in the heavenly places.

Exodus 23:31 (NKJV) And I will set your bounds from the Red Sea to the sea, Philistia, and from the desert to the River. For I will deliver the inhabitants of the land into your hand, and you shall drive them out before you.

Zechariah 12:4-5 (NKJV) "'In that day,' says the Lord, 'I will strike every horse with confusion, and its rider with madness; I will open My eyes on the house of Judah and will strike every horse of the peoples with blindness. And the governors of Judah shall say in their heart, 'The inhabitants of Jerusalem are my strength in the Lord of hosts, their God.'"

Genesis 12:3 (NKJV) I will bless those who bless you, and I will curse him who curses you; and in you all the families of the earth shall be blessed.

Isaiah 60:12 (NKJV) For the nation and kingdom which will not serve you shall perish, and those nations shall be utterly ruined.

43

COME HIGHER

I will bless those who bless you...

A Word from the Lord

My Child, from today forward, I am calling you to come higher. You ask, "What does this mean, to come higher?" It means that no matter where you are in your walk with me, there is always more of me to explore. There is more of me to get to know. There is more light available to penetrate the darkness. I am a multi-faceted God. Just as you look at a diamond, most people just look at the surface, but if you look closer, if you place a magnifying glass over it, you will see that there are more facets than you can count. That, my child, is how I am. Oh the joy I want you to experience, as you search my many facets. I am life! I am Light! I am Victory! I am Wisdom! I am Peace! I am your Comforter! Whatever you need, I AM! While you have head knowledge of all these things, you do not have heart knowledge, (Deep down spiritual heart knowledge). You are walking in a get by attitude, when you could be walking in a victory attitude. You are walking in the muck and mire instead walking in the beauty of My holiness.

The facets in a diamond make the light look like it is dancing from within. I want you to come up higher so you can experience my life dancing within you.

A diamond is brilliant, and the closer you look, the more you get to see the beauty of its brilliance. That is what I want for you. I want you to dance with me in the beauty of the light of my brilliance. Oh, how I want you to dance with me in my Word. My Word opens up layers of light that pierce any darkness you could be experiencing. To come up higher means to praise, worship and search. Praise me for what I've done, worship me for who I am and then search my layers in the depths of My word. Let Holy Spirit lead you higher. It gets brighter and more beautiful as you ascend. So, fight to ascend. Don't let distractions keep you from coming higher. In the ascension you will find great and marvelous things.

Yes Lord, I want to come higher. I want to dance in your brilliance and know you deeper. Please help me to keep ascending even when life is too busy. Help me to remember that other people need me to ascend, they need to understand who you are. I want to be light in the darkness when it tries to take over. I desire today to come up higher. I choose for my light to get brighter. I desire to worship you in the beauty of your Holiness.

In Jesus' name. Amen.

44
ACCEPT GOD'S HEALING

Woman, you are set free from your infirmity...

Luke 13:11-13 (NIV) And a woman was there who had been crippled by a spirit for eighteen years. She was bent over and could not straighten up at all. When Jesus saw her, he called her forward and said to her, "Woman, you are set free from your infirmity." Then he put his hands on her, and immediately she straightened up and praised God.

Father, thank you for this example in your Word. As I read this, it dawns on me that this woman did not come to you asking for healing, no friends brought her to you to be healed, no one was binding or loosening the enemy that you said had bound her for those eighteen years. Although all those types of healings are necessary, in this example you healed her without those things being done. How powerful your love is, Lord. She was bent over and all she could see was the ground. But you saw her, right where she was. You saw her need and healed her. She seemed to do nothing but accept her healing. Thank you, Lord, that even in my own darkness, even in my own blindness, you see me. Thank you that even if the weight of my sickness is so great that I can't even look up to search the heavens for you, You know exactly what I need, at exactly the right time. I thank you, Lord, that as I go through life you are watching me, you never leave me.

You know what I have need of before I know. Thank you, Lord, for your healing power that flows from heaven into my life and onto my family's lives. Today, I accept my healing freely just as the woman did. Thank you for touching me, Jesus, and I thank you that I hear your words "YOU ARE SET FREE FROM YOUR INFIRMITY."

In Jesus' name. 𝔄men.

45
GOD OF MIRACLES

With my whole heart, with my whole life...

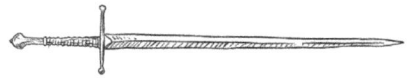

A Word from the Lord

My Child, I AM the GOD of miracles. Many of you are looking at your circumstances and saying to yourself, God no longer does miracles. I have asked for a miracle, and I don't see one. LET ME BE CLEAR; just because you do not see an immediate answer to your request for a miracle does not mean I AM not working. Your miracle could be just around the corner. Where is your faith? Does not my Word say in Hebrews 13:8 that I am the same yesterday, today and forever? You need to remember all the miracles that I performed throughout My Word. The parting of the Red Sea that destroyed my children's enemies, the woman with the issue of blood that touched the hem of My garment and was healed because of her faith, the feeding of the five thousand with just a few loaves and fish, or the miracle of friends that had faith to lower down the paralyzed man through the roof for him to be touched and healed. I placed a coin in the fish's mouth so that taxes could be paid. I need you to have the faith of the Centurion who understood authority, who understood that My Word spoken, would heal his servant. I need you to have the faith of David who understood the covenant that he had with me, the Living God! Speak My Word with faith, understanding the covenant I have with you and wait and see how I work out your miracle. I AM THE SAME GOD TODAY. I still heal the blind and cause the lame to walk. I still provide bread to the hungry and water to the thirsty. I still crush your enemy. I still calm the storms. I AM, THE GREAT I AM AND I STILL PERFORM MIRACLES. Signs and wonders happen all the time. In fact, you can see them with a few moves of your fingertips. Search them out, you will be surprised that I am moving and fulfilling My Word throughout the globe. Remember, just because you don't experience firsthand, in your time frame, doesn't mean I AM not working. Expect signs, wonders and miracles and you will see them.

Father, thank you, that you are still in the miracle business. Your Word says in *Psalm 103:1-6 (TPT) With my whole heart, with my whole life, and with my innermost being, I bow in wonder and love before you, the Holy God! Yahweh, you are my soul's celebration. How could I ever forget the miracles of kindness you've done for me? You kissed my heart with forgiveness, in spite of all I've done. You've healed me inside and out from every disease. You've rescued me from hell and saved my life. You've crowned me with love and mercy. You satisfy my every desire with good things. You've supercharged my life so that I soar again like a flying eagle in the sky! You're a God who makes things right, giving justice to the defenseless.*

Help me, Lord, to never forget your perfect absolute love. Help me to remember that you are My God, the one and only Living God who still works miracles.

PRAISE MOMENT #8

I will bless you, Lord. I will lift your name on high.
I will magnify Your name because it is great and greatly to be praised.
I will shout and sing of your goodness because you are worthy.
You are Holy. You are glorious.
Let my praise join with the symphony of voices in Heaven singing to the one and only true God.
The God of my salvation, my Deliverer, my Healer and my Victor.

Psalm 34:1-3 (KJV) I will bless the LORD at all times: His praise shall continually be in my mouth. My soul shall make her boast in the LORD: The humble shall hear thereof and be glad. O magnify the LORD with me, And let us exalt his name together.

46
POWER OF PRAYER

Watch and pray so that you will not fall into temptation...

Hebrews 4:16 (NIV) Let us then approach God's throne of grace with confidence, so that we may receive mercy and find grace to help us in our time of need.

Psalm 145:18 (NIV) The Lord is near to all who call on him, to all who call on him in truth.

Psalm 143:1 (NIV) Lord, hear my prayer, listen to my cry for mercy; in your faithfulness and righteousness come to my relief.

1 John 5:14 (NIV) This is the confidence we have in approaching God: that if we ask anything according to his will, he hears us.

Psalm 145:18 (NIV) The Lord is near to all who call on him, to all who call on him in truth.

Matthew 18:20 (NIV) For where two or three gather in my name, there am I with them.

Acts 16:25-26 (NIV) About midnight Paul and Silas were praying and singing hymns to God, and the other prisoners were listening to them. Suddenly there was such a violent earthquake that the foundations of the prison were shaken. At once all the prison doors flew open, and everyone's chains came loose.

Romans 8:26 (NIV) In the same way, the Spirit helps us in our weakness. We do not know what we ought to pray for, but the Spirit himself intercedes for us through wordless groans.

James 5:16 (NIV) Therefore confess your sins to each other and pray for each other so that you may be healed. The prayer of a righteous person is powerful and effective.

Matthew 26:41 (NIV) "Watch and pray so that you will not fall into temptation. The spirit is willing, but the flesh is weak."

2 Chronicles 7:14 (NIV) If my people, who are called by my name, will humble themselves and pray and seek my face and turn from their wicked ways, then I will hear from heaven, and I will forgive their sin and will heal their land.

A Word from the Lord

My Child, never forget that prayer is your direct communication with me. I have a covenant with you that gives you direct access to me. Prayer is your way of entering into my presence. It is your way of hearing my heartbeat. Prayer is your anchor to calm and peace in your life. When you fail to come into My presence, life gets noisy and stormy and it's hard to tune it out. Only by conversing with me can you truly tune out all the things that life and the enemy throw at you. If you pray, I can show and tell you so much as it pertains to living your best life through My Son, Jesus. I can show you which road to take when you are trying to make a decision. I can show you how to use your authority as a believer to speak victory to your situation. Not all circumstances and challenges are created equally. You must come before me and ask me how to handle any given situation. You must not leave it to chance. Do not let the hustle and bustle of life keep you out of my presence. Again, prayer is your lifeline. Every answer you need you will find in my presence. Come into my presence every day, multiple times a day. My Word says, pray without ceasing. That means to recognize that I never leave you, I am always with you, so you are able to connect to me 24/7. Take advantage of all that I have for you. Stay connected to Me.

47

HOW TO PRAY
IN THE MIDDLE OF A STORM

I will not be anxious about anything...

Father, I thank you that you are Jehovah Shalom, the God of Peace. Lord, today I am in the middle of a storm. Everything around me seems to be in chaos and turmoil. I feel as if I cannot breathe. I need you to breathe your peace upon me today. I am asking to feel your presence and your calmness. Thank you that your arms wrap around me, and you are protecting me, thank you that you are calming my fears. Thank you, that you are my Rock and my Refuge, my very help in time of trouble. I know, Lord, that you are bigger than any storm I am facing. I praise you in the middle of this storm because I know you are my God who always delivers. Give me clarity as to what I need to do, so I can get to the other side. My faith is in You and Your Word, not my feelings and senses.

In Jesus' name. Amen.

Read these verses:

Psalm 56:3 (ESV) When I am afraid, I put my trust in you.

Isaiah 41:13 (ESV) For you, the LORD my God, hold my right hand; it is You who says to me, "Fear not, I am the one who helps you."

Isaiah 43:2 (ESV) When I pass through the waters, You will be with me; and through the rivers, they shall not overwhelm me; when I walk through fire I shall not be burned, and the flame shall not consume me.

Philippians 4:6-7 (ESV) I will not be anxious about anything, but in everything by prayer and supplication with thanksgiving I will make my requests known to You. And your peace, God, which surpasses all understanding, will guard my heart and mind in Christ Jesus.

John 14:27 (ESV) Peace You leave with me; your peace You give to me. Not as the world gives do I give to you. Let not your hearts be troubled, neither let them be afraid.

Psalm 18:2 (NIV) Lord, you are my rock, my fortress and my deliverer; You, God, are my rock, in whom I take refuge, my shield and the horn of my salvation, my stronghold.

48
HELP ME GOD! I KEEP MESSING UP

Lord, you are my rock, my fortress...

A Word from the Lord

My Child, you are not alone in your feelings. My children all over the world call out to me because they feel they can't get it right. Whether it is falling back into addiction, trying to stay healthy, continuing to make the same mistakes over and over again; with family issues, business issues or personal issues, you are not alone. I know you don't feel it, but all of heaven is cheering you on. All of heaven wants you to be so connected to Me, so in tune to Me, that you see how to stop the cycle you are in. These can be hard issues. So hard in fact, that the only way out is through Me. I know you are thinking you have tried "everything"! But you have not. You have not been serious with Me. Many times, you blame others for your predicament. Ultimately, they are not to blame. You must look deep within yourself and accept that I am the only way out. You must stop dwelling on your past and realize you have a future that is bright and successful. Your issues hang over you like a dark cloud. I AM the way out; I AM the life that you desire. My truth is the light that will dispel your darkness. I do not condemn you for where you are. That is what your enemy, the devil does. I have come to give you life and give you life more abundantly, no matter what you have done. But you must let Me in, you must ask Jesus to truly be the Lord of your life and stop playing around. I know you are tired of being miserable. How many times will you get tired of saying just one more time, then I can fix it. YOU CANNOT FIX IT! Only I can deliver you and set you on a higher place. A place so high that the thing you have been struggling with will never be able to harm you again. So, connect to Me today. You have everything to gain and nothing to lose. Victory is at hand. Victory is in My hand, so reach up and grab hold of My hand RIGHT NOW!

1 John 1:9 (NIV) If we confess our sins, he is faithful and just and will forgive us our sins and purify us from all unrighteousness.

Psalm 103:12 (NIV) as far as the east is from the west, so far has he removed our transgressions from us.

2 Cor. 12:9 (NIV) But he said to me, "My grace is sufficient for you, for my power is made perfect in weakness."

Hebrew 4:16 (NIV) Let us then approach God's throne of grace with confidence, so that we may receive mercy and find grace to help us in our time of need.

Psalm 51:10 (NIV) Create in me a pure heart, O God, and renew a steadfast spirit within me.

You can't give up!!!

My Child, I need you to HEAR ME! YOU CAN NEVER GIVE UP! You must fight against the evil one. You must fight to protect your family, your Nation and your life. The enemy comes to steal, kill and destroy, but you

must fight, because I came to give you abundant life. Many of you still don't believe that Satan (the devil) exists. LOOK AROUND, do you not see all the pain and destruction. Do you not hear all the lies that he constantly spews out? Your enemy is active, he wants to wear you out. He wants you to give up. YOU CANNOT GIVE UP UNDER ANY CIRCUMSTANCES! If he can cause you or My Church to give up, he wins. If you FIGHT, you WIN! You must fight for your healing; you must fight for your family's salvation; you must fight for your children's success; you must fight for your peace! If you know Me, then you are automatically an adversary of Satan and his principalities of power and darkness. He will come after you, he will attack you at your weakest. That is why the Church is so important, you must surround each other in unity, praying for each other, edifying each other and helping each other in times of battle. There is always a battle going on. It may be your battle or someone else's, but there is always a battle going on. You need to always be in a warrior position in your prayer life, you cannot give your adversary the slightest opening. You must always have on your full armor. Your family needs you. I need you! The body of Christ, your fellow brothers and sisters need you. Put on your armor. AGAIN, NEVER GIVE UP! NEVER QUIT! Whether you choose to believe it or not LIVES DEPEND ON THE FIGHT WITHIN YOU! Stand with Me. Fight with Me. Worship Me, knowing that I am your rear guard and together in unity My church can fight the good fight of faith and overcome the evils of this world.
So put on your armor, FIGHT, UNIFY, STAND AND NEVER GIVE UP!!!!

49

PRAYING TO OVERCOME LONELINESS

Have I not commanded you? Be strong...

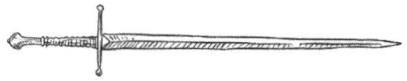

Isaiah 41:10 (NIV) So do not fear, for I am with you; do not be dismayed, for I am your God. I will strengthen you and help you; I will uphold you with my righteous right hand.

Psalm 27:10 (NIV) Though my father and mother forsake me, the Lord will receive me.

John 14:18 (NIV) I will not leave you as orphans; I will come to you.

Psalm 23:4 (NIV) Even though I walk through the darkest valley, I will fear no evil, for you are with me; your rod and your staff, they comfort me.

1 Peter 5:7 (NIV) Cast all your anxiety on him because he cares for you.

Joshua 1:9 (NIV) Have I not commanded you?Be strong and courageous. Do not be afraid; do not be discouraged, for the LORD your God will be with you wherever you go.

𝕱ather, today I have an overwhelming feeling of loneliness. I feel isolated. I feel like screaming, but I know no one will hear me. Life feels like it's in slow motion, it feels as if there is no way out of the depression I am experiencing. Lately, on most days I let my loneliness define me. Friends and family seem to be far off, out of reach. In a world of 8 billion people, why am I lonely?

A Word from the Lord

My Child, the loneliness you feel is not due to lack of people in your life, for you engage with people every day. The loneliness you feel is due to the lack of knowledge you have about me. I am truly the only one who can fill those lonely places in your heart. I AM the companion you seek. I AM the One you need to be conversing with, because I AM your everything. You listen to what the world says. You listen to what other people say about you. You even listen to what you say about yourself, BUT you fail to listen to Me. You must search My Word. It is clear in Deut. 3:16 Be strong and courageous. Do not fear or be in dread of them, for it is Me, the Lord your God, who goes with you. I WILL NOT LEAVE YOU OR FORSAKE YOU! My Child, you must concentrate on the fact that I am always with you. I will never leave you. Even if everyone seems against you. I AM RIGHT BY YOUR SIDE! Even if you are walking THROUGH the SHADOW of death, know that I am with you and I am comforting you. You must tap into who I AM. I AM the greatest resource you have in order to overcome this loneliness and isolation you feel. Isolation is a tactic of your enemy, the devil. He wants you to feel alone. So, when the waves of loneliness roll in, picture my loving arms around you. The moment loneliness tries to creep in, picture Me telling you, it will all be OK, just focus on ME. Cast all your anxieties on me because I care for you. Fear not loneliness and isolation because I am with you; be not dismayed, for I am your God; I will strengthen you, I will help you, I will uphold you with my righteous right hand. It doesn't matter who comes and goes in and out of your life. I AM RIGHT WITH YOU, WHEREVER YOU ARE!

Thank you, Lord, for understanding my feelings. Thank you for reminding me that you are my source in everything. Please impress upon me to picture you, just as you described. I choose to see you, MY GOD, with your loving arms wrapped around me, telling me, I'll be OK. I choose to search your Word for the comfort and answers I need. I choose to block out the enemy's voice with your Word. I choose to replace my thoughts of loneliness with your thoughts of overcoming. I choose your words over my words, thoughts and feelings.

In Jesus' name. Amen.

50
OVERCOMING OBSTACLES

The light shines in the darkness...

Father, today I have what seems like a giant standing in my way. An obstacle so large that it seems insurmountable. I know your Word says in Proverbs 3:5-6 - Trust in the LORD with all my heart, and do not lean on my own understanding. In all my ways acknowledge You and you will make straight my paths. I know you direct my path. I know you are right here with me. I know you see exactly what I am facing, and you have the answer on how to overcome and defeat this giant. Thank you, Jesus, that I can speak your word to any giant and have great expectation of victory. So today I speak your Word to my giant.

Speak these personalized scriptures over yourself until your giant is defeated.

John 16:33 (NIV) Jesus, you say these things to me, that in you I may have peace. In the world I will have tribulation. But I take heart, because you have overcome the world.

Romans 8:28 (NIV) And I know that in all things God, You work for the good of those who love you, who have been called according to your purpose.

2 Cor. 4:8 (NIV) I am hard pressed on every side, but not crushed; perplexed, but not in despair; persecuted, but not abandoned; struck down, but not destroyed.

1 Peter 5:10 (NIV) And you, the God of all grace, who called me to your eternal glory in Christ, after I have suf-

fered a little while, you will restore me and make me strong, firm and steadfast.

John 14:27 (NIV) Peace you leave with me; your peace you give me. You do not give to me as the world gives. I will not let my heart be troubled and I will not be afraid.

Phil. 4:6-7 (NIV) I will not be anxious about anything, but in every situation, by prayer and petition, with thanksgiving, present my requests to you, God. And your peace, which transcends all understanding, will guard my heart and my mind in Christ Jesus.

1 John 5:4 (NIV) For everyone born of you, God, overcomes the world. This is the victory that has overcome the world, even my faith.

John 1:5 (NIV) The light shines in the darkness, and the darkness has not overcome it.

1 John 4:4 (NIV) You, dear children, are from God and have overcome, because the one who is in you is greater than the one who is in the world.

Psalm 23:4 (NIV) Even though I walk through the darkest valley, I will fear no evil, for you are with me; your rod and your staff, they comfort me.

Isaiah 40:31 (NIV) I will wait upon you Lord and will renew my strength. I shall mount up with wings as eagles; I will run and not be weary, and I shall walk and not faint.

Prov. 24:10 (NIV) If I falter in a time of trouble, how small is my strength!

Psalm 34:19 (NIV) The righteous person may have many troubles, but you LORD deliver me from them all.

Zech. 4:6 (ESV) Then you said, "This is the word of the Lord to Zerubbabel: Not by might, nor by power, but by my Spirit, says the Lord of Hosts."

51
HEARING GOD'S VOICE

For the word of God is living and active....

Father, my deepest desire is to hear your voice. Help me to remember that when I renew my mind with your Word, which is perfect truth, I can know that you are always speaking to me. I am asking that your Voice invade my life, and that I hear you over the noise and chaos that so often surrounds me. I choose to allow your still, small voice to pierce all other conversations. Let your voice be the loudest voice I hear. I choose to speak your Word over all situations in my life because it is a light unto my path. Thank you for your promise that if I call out to you, you will hear me and that you will answer me. Help me search your Word, which will pave the way to hearing you speak to me. Lord, thank you that the Holy Spirit teaches me all things and brings to my remembrance all that you have said to me. Thank you, that I can come boldly to the throne of grace and expect to hear your voice. Thank you that I can confirm the Word I hear with the written Word to ensure I am hearing correctly. Continue to teach me your ways as I search your depths. I will hear your voice. Thank you for your love that endures forever.

In Jesus' name. Amen.

Isaiah 30:21 (NIV) Whether you turn to the right or to the left, your ears will hear a voice behind you, saying, "This is the way; walk in it."

Jeremiah 33:3 (NIV) Call to me and I will answer you and tell you great and unsearchable things you do not know.

Psalm 85:8 (NKJ) Let me hear what God the LORD will speak, for he will speak peace to his people, to his saints; but let them not turn back to folly.

Psalm 119:105 (NIV) Your word is a lamp to my feet and a light to my path.

John 8:47 (NKJV) Whoever is of God hears the words of God. The reason why you do not hear them is that you are not of God.

John 10:16 (NKJV) And I have other sheep that are not of this fold. I must bring them also, and they will listen to my voice. So, there will be one flock, one shepherd.

John 10:27 (NKJV) My sheep hear my voice, and I know them, and they follow me.

John 14:26 (NKJV) But the Helper, the Holy Spirit, whom the Father will send in my name, he will teach you all things and bring to your remembrance all that I have said to you.

John 16:13 (NKJV) When the Spirit of truth comes, he will guide you into all the truth, for he will not speak on his own authority, but whatever he hears he will speak, and he will declare to you the things that are to come.

Hebrews 2:11 (NJKV) Therefore we must pay much closer attention to what we have heard, lest we drift away from it.

Hebrews 4:12 (NKJV) For the word of God is living and active, sharper than any two-edged sword, piercing to the division of soul and of spirit, of joints and of marrow, and discerning the thoughts and intentions of the heart.

Rev. 3:20 (NKJV) Behold, I stand at the door and knock. If anyone hears my voice and opens the door, I will come in to him and eat with him, and he with me.

52

CONFIDENCE IN VICTORY

You come against me with sword and spear and javelin...

A Word from the Lord

My child, as you grow in me there comes a birthing of confidence. Confidence that My Word is perfect, and it ALWAYS accomplishes what it says. Confidence that I AM YOUR GOD and with Me, nothing is impossible. I want you to understand that as David was facing Goliath, he was confident that I would give him victory, even though the giant he was facing was massive. Keep in mind, he wasn't just facing the giant; he was facing the entire Philistine army. David knew that through Me he had killed a lion and a bear. He felt my strength rise up in him. The more he relied on Me, the deeper His understanding of me grew. I prepared David along the way, so that when it came time for him to go up against the giant, he would have the confidence to do so. That is exactly what I am doing with you. It's time for you to be bold, just like David. David said to Goliath in 1 Samuel 17:45-47, "You come against me with sword and spear and javelin, but I come against you in the name of the Lord Almighty, the God of the armies of Israel, whom you have defied. This day the Lord will deliver you into my hands, and I'll strike you down and cut off your head. This very day I will give the carcasses of the Philistine army to the birds and the wild animals, and the whole world will know that there is a God in Israel. All those gathered here will know that it is not by sword or spear that the Lord saves; for the battle is the Lord's, and he will give all of you into our hands." I am no respecter of persons. The same way I delivered David, I WILL DELIVER YOU! The giant that you are facing right now is not bigger than I AM, I don't care what it is. I AM bigger than your greatest giant. I AM bigger than any sickness or disease, I AM bigger than your greatest heartache, I AM bigger than anything the enemy can throw at you. Nothing is more powerful than I AM. I need you to be confident that you can face your giant and proclaim that you come in the name of the Lord Almighty, the God of Israel and this day you have the victory. Speak to your giant with confidence that YOU WIN because I AM your God in whom you trust, and the shed blood of Jesus defeats your giant. And remember the deeper you dive into Me the greater your confidence grows.

ABOUT *THEDA*

Theda Vaughan is a passionate and devoted follower of Jesus Christ, making her literary debut with ***Warrior Prayers* Conversations with God**.

She lives in Greenville, SC with her husband Ricky, two sons, one daughter, two daughter-in-laws and two grandchildren. She is a businesswoman who desires to see the absolute love of God shared throughout the world. She has traveled extensively abroad sharing God's love and, through those experiences, she has continued to develop her prayer life; she is always learning to hear God's voice in a greater way.

Over the years Theda has been inspired by seeing how God has moved in her life and the lives of others through prayer. Theda has experienced a divine healing encounter and has seen her and her husband's businesses rescued. Seeing these things and many other miraculous works by God has strengthened and inspired her prayer life.

Her divine healing came from praying in faith and believing it was God's desire for her to be healed. God arranged an event for her to have faith filled leaders pray for her by the laying on of hands, but she states, that because of her diligence in praying and not giving up on the Word of God, God orchestrated her healing. Theda and her husband Ricky have grown businesses and watched God see them through the selling of one business, blessing them financially and watching their resources dry up while going through the great recession in 2009. But with prayer, coupled with faith, God brought them out on the other side. She has seen God's miracle working power through prayer work repeatedly. The prayers in this book are the types of prayers she and her husband have prayed over the years with results. She desires the reader to connect intimately with the Father, Jesus and Holy Spirit, hearing the voice of the Father clearly while understanding the absolute love of God through Jesus. Theda wants the reader to understand that only through prayer and communication with God can you live the abundant life you desire.

> The greatest trick the Devil ever pulled was convincing the world he didn't exist.
>
> CHARLES BAUDELAIRE

Thank you for praying
Warrior Prayers Conversations with God
by Theda Vaughan!

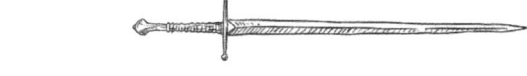

If this prayer book inspired you to *engage the Lord even more*, please consider leaving a review on the listing of purchase.
This small gesture helps in a BIG way to share the goodness of God!
Thank you so much!
Be sure to follow **Take Heart Books** on FB to encounter more Christian authors spreading the Gospel of Jesus Christ!

To reach Theda Vaughan, send an email to
theda@warriorprayerbooks.com

If you wish to purchase in bulk for your prayer or bible study group, please contact Theda at
theda@warriorprayerbooks.com

www.ingramcontent.com/pod-product-compliance
Lightning Source LLC
Chambersburg PA
CBHW020904090426
42736CB00008B/494